AF287307

EUL VERLAG

EINZELSCHRIFTEN

Thomas Eschenbach
Zum Budgetdefizitkriterium des Stabilitäts- und Wachstumspaktes
Lohmar – Köln 2010 ◆ 200 S. ◆ € 49,- (D) ◆ ISBN 978-3-89936-932-8

Marco Dreher
Unternehmenswertorientiertes Beteiligungscontrolling –
Aufgabenspezifische Fundierung auf Basis entscheidungs- und
kapitalmarktorientierter Konzepte der Unternehmensbewertung
Lohmar – Köln 2010 ◆ 556 S. ◆ € 76,- (D) ◆ ISBN 978-3-89936-933-5

Laura Gerardy, Johannes Vogel, Leif Chr. Steinbrinker und Sybille Falke
Zukunftsmodell Ärztenetzwerke – Eine empirische Untersuchung der Auswirkungen auf die Healthcare Industrie
Lohmar – Köln 2010 ◆ 120 S. ◆ € 42,- (D) ◆ ISBN 978-3-89936-934-2

Marco Vietor
Studienfinanzierung durch Humankapitalverträge – Eine
Marktanalyse
Lohmar – Köln 2010 ◆ 200 S. ◆ € 49,- (D) ◆ ISBN 978-3-89936-935-9

Henning Struck
**Mandatsunfähigkeit von Aufsichtsratsmitgliedern einer
deutschen Aktiengesellschaft**
Lohmar – Köln 2010 ◆ 252 S. ◆ € 57,- (D) ◆ ISBN 978-3-89936-937-3

Richard Vahrenkamp
The German Autobahn 1920–1945 – Hafraba Visions and
Mega Projects
Lohmar – Köln 2010 ◆ 280 S. ◆ € 58,- (D) ◆ ISBN 978-3-89936-940-3

Thorsten Korn, Gregor van der Beek und Eva Fischer (Hrsg.)
Aktuelle Herausforderungen in der Wirtschaftsförderung –
Chancen und Perspektiven in einer sich wandelnden Welt
Lohmar – Köln 2010 ◆ 208 S. ◆ € 49,- (D) ◆ ISBN 978-3-89936-942-7

Frank Bezjak
**Global Economic Trends and their Impact to Corporate
Development**
Lohmar – Köln 2010 ◆ 116 S. ◆ € 41,- (D) ◆ ISBN 978-3-89936-943-4

JOSEF EUL VERLAG

Frank Bezjak

Global Economic Trends and their Impact to Corporate Development

With a Preface by Prof. Dr. Eric Frère,
FOM Hochschule für Ökonomie & Management, Essen

Bibliografische Information der Deutschen Nationalbibliothek

Die Deutsche Nationalbibliothek verzeichnet diese Publikation
in der Deutschen Nationalbibliografie; detaillierte bibliografische
Daten sind im Internet über <http://dnb.d-nb.de> abrufbar.

ISBN 978-3-89936-943-4
1. Auflage Juli 2010

© JOSEF EUL VERLAG GmbH, Lohmar – Köln, 2010
Alle Rechte vorbehalten

JOSEF EUL VERLAG GmbH
Brandsberg 6
53797 Lohmar
Tel.: 0 22 05 / 90 10 6-6
Fax: 0 22 05 / 90 10 6-88
E-Mail: info@eul-verlag.de
http://www.eul-verlag.de

**Bei der Herstellung unserer Bücher möchten wir die Umwelt schonen. Dieses
Buch ist daher auf säurefreiem, 100% chlorfrei gebleichtem, alterungsbeständigem Papier nach DIN 6738 gedruckt.**

Preface

Global Economic Trends or Megatrends have a profound influence for the strategic planning process of corporate development units. There are myriad reasons for this.

Due to a reduced time of stability in today's business, volatility and competition increase.   As an outcome, corporations need to enhance their change management processes in relation to the new value configuration of markets. Latter can also be perceived as a shift of paradigm in the way that business is conducted. Furthermore, a fast changing environment is challenging for corporations, who need to adapt quickly to the new business situation in order to stay competitive, or simply to avoid harm to the corporation. Therefore, the main interest of strategic planners is how can perceive and measure these trends to develop effective countermeasures that protect the corporation. Indeed, this problem definition is of complex nature.

The deliverables of Frank Bezjak's master thesis can be summed up as follows. This book delivers valuable insights on the functional chain from underlying causes of Global Economic Trends to their impact to corporations. This is done by introducing the main key performance indicators that measure market activity, as well as, by introducing the concept on how to align these indicators for strategic decision-making. To demonstrate the theory, the top seven Global Economic Trends of the 21st century are introduced.

A practical toolset, which is derived from the theory, is the core scientific contribution of this work. It can be used to estimate the possible impact of a global economic trend to corporations, and to establish countermeasures. A practical case study with the focus on the scarcity of resources and their impact to the chemical industry rounds off the introduced concept. This case study is conducted with Bayer to show the practical applicability of the theory.

The theory is derived from various fields of knowledge, which are strongly related to the field of corporate development. In detail, tools and concepts such as value based management, portfolio management, strategic management, or change management are combined to deliver a solid theoretical foundation for the analysis. An additional aspect of this work is the incorporation of knowledge management into the strategic planning process. The idea of the author is to make the planning process as effective as possible, by incorporating all strategic levels of the corporation into the planning process.

The presented Master Dissertation combines existing literature in a new way and extends it in some parts. Considering the aspect that Frank Bezjak has written this dissertation beneath his work in a short amount of time, the results are reasonable and applicable.

Many of the aspects presented can be directly integrated into the daily work of corporations. This work is another example that attaining an excellent academic level is not exclusively possible under the conditions of a full-time MBA program. Nevertheless, part-time concepts as the FOM MBA program make high demands on their participants. Consistent discipline and the ability to self-motivation are the key skills to cope with the challenges of graduating alongside a career – attributes characterizing people with long-term success.

Prof Dr. Eric Frère

Head of Corporate Finance and International Entrepreneurship,

Dean of FOM Graduate School

Foreword

In this volatile world, there are substantial uncertainties over future economic growth, arising from the complex interplay of domestic and global determinants. Global Economic Trends have sustainably changed today's economic and socioeconomic landscape, and the transformational power of GETs will drive industries and markets to a new secular destination.

Without a doubt, Global Economic Trends are a very interesting and wide field of research. This topic has caught my interest from the very beginning of my MBA program. But, there is not much scientific literature at hand about Global Economic Trends, as well as, Corporate Development. Latter is mostly illustrated within strategic management books, but not exposed separately. My goal with this thesis was to give students, and business people, a broad overview about this topic, as well as, to provide pragmatic approach. Because of its complexity, providing full-blown theoretical groundwork was not possible, and would be equal to opening Pandora's Box. Therefore, the focus of this work is to give the reader an overview of this topic, and to show how to identify, and to align the right information to successfully conduct strategic decision-making.

Corporations need to establish organizational measures to incorporate Global Economic Trends into the strategic management process, and to avoid harm to the corporate portfolio, and to defend their strategic position. Therefore, the analysis of Global Economic Trends is especially challenging, when addressing long-term resource and investment decisions. The scientific core of this thesis is a framework contributed called GET Assessment framework can be applied within strategic business planning to tackle risks associated to GETs. The intent of the tool is to analyze the impact of a trend to the actual business situation of the corporation, and to help the management to formulate and to establish counter measures within a scenario planning.

To prove its applicability, a case study is conducted. The GET scarcity of resources is used to demonstrate how the shortage of oil is affecting a virtual corporation that is operating within the chemical industry, which is a recent problem to business planning in the industry. Using the concept of corporate evaluation, which is introduced within the assessment framework, potential risks are identified. By this means, external risks are mapped to the internal environment of the corporation. Then countermeasures are developed, which protect the virtual corporation. This approach is straight forward and helps to perceive possible future scenarios, which is useful for student who approach this topic, as well as, practitioners, who seek for new ideas.

Even though that there is only one author on the cover, there are many people in the back that helped giving birth to this book. First, I would like to thank Prof Dr. Eric Frère, Dean of FOM Graduate School, for giving me the chance to write this academic thesis and to provide help where necessary. Since the first academic semester, I enjoyed his outspoken and highly motivating teaching methods. For the case study of this book, I would like to thank Dr. Beate Degen, Head of Corporate Strategy Projects at Bayer, for helping me to establish a real scenario. As if by chance, the scarcity of resources, especially oil, is a topic that even became more important due to the accident of BP in the Gulf of Mexico.

Finally, I would like to address some personal matters. When you are involved in international projects, conducting an MBA beside a job is tough duty. This can be very stressful and pushes you to personal limits. Even though, I am very thankful for the experience and knowledge that I have gained from this study program.

This book is dedicated to my family and beloved ones. First, I would like thank my mom and dad Darinka and Josef Bezjak for supporting me during this tough time. Without your altruistic help, this project would be a failure. Finally, yet importantly, I would like to thank all of my colleagues and friends, who supported me during this tough time, and who tolerated my moods.

Frank Bezjak

Table of Content

List of figures

List of Tables

Abbreviations

%	Percent
$	Dollar
bn	billion
BU	Business Unit
CD	Corporate Development
CEO	Chief Executive Officer
CM	Change Management
COP15	15th United Nations Climate Change Conference in Copenhagen
Cp.	Compare
CPI	Consumer Price Index
CS	Corporate Strategy
CSR	Corporate Social Responsibility
DCF	Discounted Cash Flow
e.g.	exempli gratia [Latin]: for example
EMH	Efficient markets hypothesis
EVA	Earned Value Added
FCF	Free Cash Flow
FDA	Federal Drug Association
FDI	Foreign direct investments
GDP	Gross Domestic Product
GMP	Good Manufacturing Practices
GNP	Gross Nation Product
IEA	International Energy Agency
IMF	International Monetary Fund
KM	Knowledge Management
M&A	Mergers and Acquisitions
MNC	Multinational Companies

NOPAT	Net Operating Profit after Tax
OECD	Organization for Economic Co-operation and Development
OPEC	Organization of the Petroleum Exporting Countries
SBU	Strategic Business Unit
SME	Small and Medium Enterprises
SWF	Sovereign wealth funds
tn	Trillion
VC	Virtual Company
WACC	Weighted average cost of capital
IPCC	Intergovernmental Panel on Climate Change

1   Introduction

1.1   Problem Definition

Today, business firms do not only face increasing competition in their markets and for their inputs, but also heavy macroeconomic driving forces the so-called megatrends or global economic trends. These trends deeply transform markets and have a certain impact to corporations. Even though, the dilemma is that the new destination is mostly unknown to manager within an organization, but corporations need to implement change measures quickly in order to avoid harm to the organization. These circumstances raise the degree of uncertainty for business planning and directly influence the risk factor of the corporate portfolio. The portfolio risk is a key driver for company strategists, and therefore the economic changes are a key challenge for global corporate development of an organization.[1]

Consequently, companies have to be prepared to change in no time, but it is increasingly difficult to predict what exactly will happen next. Therefore, companies need to hold change capacity within the organization. In short, they need to be prepared that changes will occur, and may not have much time to change. This is especially difficult in large corporations that operate globally. Planning and execution of a wide range of strategic activities and initiatives are at the heart of corporate development. Change management is an approach to lock in the strategic targets for the executives who conduct the change process within the organization. The question is how the theoretical approaches of change management can be applied to hit the strategic targets most efficiently. The discipline of Change Management addresses the process of change within the organization, but the belief or the assumption that change is manageable leads to faulty interventions, according to Michael Jarrett.[2]

For example, frame-breaking change involves a new definition of the companies' core values, (b) an alteration of the distribution of power, (c) a modification in structure, systems and procedures, or (d) change in the way that people work together within the organization.[3] It is obvious that these measures are extremely difficult to conduct, and require enormous discipline by the people who are leading the change. Furthermore, the corporate environment has to provide the capabilities to be changeable.

---

[1] Cf. Kottler (2002), p. 32
[2] Cf. Crainer (2004), p. 834
[3] Cf. Nilakant (2007), p. 47

Thus, the classical approaches of change management need to be refined to fit in the context of the organization. Even more, changes to the organization need to be inline with the values of the corporation. Without this strategic fit, changes will not be effective and can cause serious harm to the corporation. This leads to the question how does a model of change management look like in regard to corporate development, and how can it be applied within the organizational context to tackle the challenges of global economic trends. If a model can be found during the analysis, then its applicability has to be proven.

The problem statement clearly indicates that there are several issues attached to the topic of Global Economic Trends and their impact to corporate development. The following table reveals these issues.

No.	Problem statements
1	New economic developments challenge the global economy, as we know it today. What factors or trends are shaping the economy of tomorrow?
2	How do economic changes affect the portfolio of a company?
3	How can companies handle the volatility of risk? What are the basic concepts in terms of financial risk?
4	How does change management help to implement the measures to handle the volatility of the risk? How does this concept fit into the context of corporate development? Is there a potential to develop an individual model, and if so, what does this model look like?
5	What is the general status quo of change management? What are most famous tools and frameworks that are used? How is change management applied for global corporate development?

Table 1: Problem statements of the analysis

1.2   Objectives

The main objective of this thesis is to give the reader a holistic view how the methodologies of risk analysis and change management can be into incorporated into the strategic planning process to tackle the risks associated to GETs.

Several objectives can be formulated to solve the main objective, defined above. In regard to the problem statements defined in 1.1., an unique objective is assigned to each of the depicted problems. By this method, an individual knowledge gap can be defined for each problem. During the analysis, each of the objectives, which is depicted below, tries to be solved.

No.	Objectives
1	Evaluate the crucial driving factors that are shaping the macroeconomics and the corporate development of tomorrow. Identify the top seven global economic trends.
2	Demonstrate the impact of the economic changes to the portfolio of a company.
3	Illustrate the status quo corporate development, including the concepts and tools that are applied to analyze the actual position and the risk situation.
4	Develop or apply a change management framework that is capable to tackle the change of the economic landscape. Encompass risk management, and show how it can be implemented in global corporate development.
5	Show how the management framework can be applied to one of the economic driving factors. Take the shortage of oil, as a macroeconomic driving factor, and show how it is affecting the portfolio risk of the company.

Table 2: Objectives

1.3   Methodology

The methodology applied within the analysis is manifold. In the first chapter, the top seven global economic trends are revealed, and their economical, financial, social, and ecological effect is depicted. Based on desktop research, sources from professional consulting companies, journals, and scientific books are utilized to reason the analysis. These trends lay the foundation for further reasoning, especially for the impact on corporations. The direction of these trends and their impact on corporations is also depicted within the first chapter, but it is refined in the further analysis.

The intent of chapter is to give the reader a holistic view on how global economic trends affect corporations, and how Corporate Development can apply change management strategies to establish countermeasures that tackle the associated risks that arise out of a GET.

First, the concepts of strategic planning, portfolio management, and value-based management are illustrated to show how exactly global economic trends are affecting the corporation, and where the risks have to be taken into account. By this means, impact to corporations is pinpointed.

Second, a tool called GET assessment framework is developed that can be applied within strategic business planning to tackle the associated risks. The foundation for this framework is developed from desktop research, especially by incorporating literature from the field of risk and change management. The tool provides both, the analysis of the corporate environment and the business situation, and the execution of counter measures to tackle the impact of global economic trends.

To prove the academic analysis, the toolset is applied in form of a case study, based on the global economic trend called "scarcity of resources". This is done in corporation with the Bayer AG. In detail, the scarcity of oil is used to demonstrate the effect on the corporation and to demonstrate how a virtual corporation that is operating within the chemical industry can establish counter measures for the short-term and long-term business planning. The case study is limited to the point where the counter measures are written down. The implementation of change measures according to the change management measures is not shown within the analysis.

2   Global Economic Trends

Before the global financial crisis, economic growth seemed to be robust and rising without any interference. However, there are substantial uncertainties over future economic growth arising from the complex interplay of domestic and global determinants, including such diverse factors as demographics, advances in technology, capital availability, commodity prices, domestic policies and global trade, regimes, environmental policies and financial regulations.[4] These new forces have sustainably changed today's economic and socioeconomic landscape and set the trends for the future development. Under the umbrella term Global Economic Trends (GETs), these trends are analyzed. This chapter reveals the top seven GETs for the 21st century, shows how they can be measured, determines their impact, and distinguishes them from market noise.

2.1   Definition of a Global Economic Trend

A trend, by definition is a general direction in which a condition, output, or process, or an average or general tendency of a series of data points is developing or changing over time.[5] In this regard, an economic trend can be defined as the direction how the economy will change. Therefore, a global economic trend, further called GET, is the dynamic force that is changing the global economy. Another expression for global economic trend is megatrend. John Naisbitt made this term popular in 1982 in his bestseller Megatrends - Ten New Directions Transforming our Lives.[6] Both definitions consider that a trend is more then a measurable or visible market effect. It is rather a paradigm shift.

A paradigm is a set of rational behavior, tacit or explicit knowledge, which influences people's decision-making processes on existing problems.[7] Metaphorically speaking, it may be perceived as the hidden force that is driving peoples thinking and action taking. Concerning global economic trends, this hidden force can be political, social, financial, environmental, or macro-economical. These changes can also be referred as secular transformations, which are fundamental, sustainable, and long-term.[8] These phenomena affect the potency of investment strategies and influence the effectiveness of risk management approaches. Yet, there is no a priori knowledge of the impact of these forces to corporations available.

---

[4] Cf. Opec (2006), p. 5
[5] Cf. Business Dictionary (2010)
[6] Cf. Rust (2008), p.85
[7] Cf. The Free Dictionary (2010)
[8] Cf. El-Erian (2008), p. viii

As Peter Drucker stated, every organization operates on a theory of business, which is a set of assumptions or paradigms.[9] Global Economic trends have a huge impact on e.g. economic growth, wealth, inflation, or investment returns. They have an environmental, economical, and financial effect on all industries, nations, societies, as well as, the environment.

The question is if the past economic paradigms have been built upon a steady development of the economy, does the new development change the paradigms of business. Therefore, the assumption is that global economic trends will affect the development of international macroeconomics, and will lead to a paradigm change.[10] If so, global leaders in governments, organizations, institutions, industries, and companies will have to reshape their strategy, in order to stay competitive in the future business environment.

Knowing the underlying constraints and the impact of GETs is consequently for investors on all levels, because the effect of these trends can be devastating to existing businesses. As an example, the burst of the financial bubble in 2007 has become famous as the subprime crisis, which led to a global recession. Concerning the author Nassim Nicholas Taleb, this event is also called a black swan event.[11] In his notes, this term is a synonym for an unknown event with a devastating impact, which is not perceivable ex-ante. The author refers such events as the unknown-unknown; in relation to Karl Popper's philosophic theories, he postulates that to be able to predict the future, "you need to incorporate elements from this future itself".[12] El-Erian characterizes these trends by stating, "they appear to be difficult to fully identify and comprehend, and involve changes in both mature and emerging financial markets."[13] Hence, economic theory and economic policy are unlikely to be effective by themselves in a period of change.[14] E.g., the efficient-markets hypothesis (EMH) postulates, that deviation from equilibrium could not last long.[15] The indirect consequence is that bubbles could not form, or last. Both, the direct and the indirect effect of the EMH are not valid in times of crisis and uncertainty. Myron Scholes, who in 1997 won the Nobel Prize in economics, says the blame for recent woe should be pinned on Wall Street investors, not on economic theorists.[16]

Therefore, global economic trends do change the existing paradigms of business theory. In this regard it can be postulated that the theory can only be as good as it

---

[9] Cf. Drucker (2007), p. 36
[10] Cf. ECB (2009)
[11] Cf. Taleb (2007), pp.33
[12] Cf. Taleb (2007), p.172
[13] Cf. El-Erian (2008), p. VII
[14] Cf. Drucker (2007), p.80
[15] Cf. The Economist (2009 a), p.71
[16] Cf. The Economist (2009 a), p.72

application. To complete the analysis concerning Black swans, Taleb describes such a state of transformation with his model of "Exstremistan", where e.g. future development is hard to predict from past information, and the environment is vulnerable to unpredictable black swans.[17] Therefore, investors need to be aware that unpredictable events occur more often in a time of market transformation.

2.2   Trends vs. market noise

Scientifically, noise is a term for unqualified back and forth movement of a value in a short period, without an actual fundamental change. If it continues in a certain direction, it will become a trend, which is the indication of the general direction of the market.[18] As secular transformations gather momentum on two of the most global markets of the world, the financial and the energy market, all businesses that are associated with these markets tend to volatile reactions, which produce market noise. If noise is perceived as important and influencing financial assets of a company, then the methodology is to observe and to analyze the development based on financial and economical methods to identify the underlying causes of the noise. The outcome of the analysis should be a short-term and a long-term scenario that predict the development of affected assets.[19] Otherwise, the noise should simply be ignored, to avoid overreaction, which may lead to wrong investment decisions.[20]

The main finding of El-Erian regarding noise is that it is "signaling the emergence of deep and, as yet, little-understood changes impacting the global economic and financial landscape".[21] This leads to the fact that the global financial investment world of today suffers from simultaneous inconsistencies. Rather than just being inconsistent over time, the progressively louder signals coming from various market segments also became increasingly inconsistent at the same time.[22] Hence, the underlying effects of market development are harder to clarify, because future development is hard to predict from past information. Therefore, corporate strategists need to seek for information about secular transformations to identify the forces that are dominating the market development. This has be achieved by steady monitoring the development of trends.

---

[17] Cf. Taleb (2007), p.36
[18] Cf. Investopedia (2010)
[19] El-Erian (2009), p.8
[20] De Bondt (2007), p. 794
[21] El-Erian (2009), p.8
[22] El Erian (2009), p. 9

2.3   Identification and measurability of global economic trends

Before the next chapter reveals the main global economic trends, the methodology of the analysis is presented. In order to identify and to measure economic trends (a) economic indicators, (b) financial indicators, and (c) ecological indicators need to be considered to illustrate the as-is and the will-be situation. However, it must be stated here that the final secular destination, the new equilibrium, is still unknown. At this point the important indicator from the fields from the economics, macroeconomics and microeconomics, which are used within the analysis, are illustrated.

2.3.1 Economical Indicators

From the macroeconomic perspective, both the gross domestic product (GDP) and the gross national product (GNP) both indicate the economic wealth of a nation. The gross national product measures the final output or expenditure of nation owned factors or production, whether they are domestic or overseas. Further, it includes the GDP, which values the productivity within the geographical boundaries of a country.[23] There are two types of GDP. Nominal GDP uses current prices to evaluate the productivity of a nation, whereas real GDP shows the production of goods and services valued at constant prices. Latter gives information about the long-term development of a nation, because it just shows productivity, without changes in price.[24] Furthermore, GDP includes the unemployment rate of a country. GDP growth from period to period results in a falling unemployment rate. The national output is higher, and, hence, more laborers keep greater levels of production.[25] Last, but not least, inflation rate and the Consumer Price index (CPI) represents the development of prices. With these indicators, a reasonable forecast of the upcoming supply and demand situation is possible.

2.3.2 Financial indicators

To gain a deeper understanding of the global driving forces that shape the financial landscape, markets should be analyzed, as well as, investment behavior of corporations. On international financial markets various type of paper assets such as equities (shares), government debt (bills, bond, etc.), resource price indices, financial derivates (options, etc.), and foreign exchange are traded.[26]

---

[23] Cf. Riley (2009)
[24] Cf. Mankiw (2008), p. 213
[25] Cf. Investopedia (2010)
[26] Cf. Wall (2004), p. 2

To measure these market activities, various indicators, such as exchange rates, stock market indices, yield curves, and interest rates, should be assessed.

Even more important, especially for the in-depth analysis of the shift of power from developed economies to emerging economies, is the Foreign Direct Investment (FDI) indicator. [27] It measures the inward and outward investment activity of companies, as well as nations, who use Sovereign Wealth Funds (SWF) as their investment vehicle. The inward FDI shows the investments that are done within a country from the outside. Therefore, the inward FDI of Germany shows how many investments are done from foreign countries. In the opposite direction, the outward FDI of Germany illustrates how many investments Germany does into other economies. The investments can be direct, for example by building a production site in another country or indirect when a company directly invests into an existing production of another country, either by buying shares or bonds. Latter is associated with Mergers and Acquisitions (M&A). A valuable data resource for these indicators is the International Monetary Found (IMF).

2.3.3 Environmental indicators

The ecological impact of a GET is the most complicated assessment. It focuses more on the technical aspects then on economical aspects. Used within this analysis is the development of the total output of carbon dioxide, which is the concentration of gases defined as parts per million.[28] This measure is widely accepted as a value to indicate pollution in relation to their carbon dioxide emissions.

In short, Corporations have a maximum capacity how much carbon dioxide they are allowed to emit. If this maximum is reached, they can buy further emission certificates, which allow them to emit more carbon dioxide, or also sulphur dioxide, or nitric oxide. The global carbon project (GCP) is a research project that quantifies, attributes, and predicts the development the evolution of the carbon cycle and is valid source for information. The global aspect of pollution is cover by incorporating the increase in global temperature, as well as, the rise of sea levels.

Within the case study of this thesis, the scarcity of oil is analyzed exemplary. The measure used within this context is mega barrel per day. This measure indicates the capacity of oil. Because oil is a raw material that is gained from nature, this measure is also perceived as an environmental indicator.

---

[27] Cf. Canadell (2003)
[28] Cf. The Economist (2009 b), p.4

2.4   Types of global economic trends

As the previous analysis showed how GETs can be identified and measured, this chapter reveals the top seven global economic trends for the 21st century. The following figure depicts the trends and their effects, which are analyzed within this subchapter.

No	Global Economic Trend	Effect
1	Collapsing Birthrate in the developed world	• Negative Effect on the GDP • Rising Costs for healthcare • Replacement of fertility • Problem to find expert personal
2	Climate Change	• CO_2 production is too high • Rise of the world temperature • Rise of the sea level
3	Shift of power from developed economies to emerging economies	• Emerging economies will be the backbone of the financial market of tomorrow • New type of investors will dictate global trends
4	Changing financial landscape	• Economic growth will be volatile • New type of investors will dictate the investment trends • Emerging economies are the net provider of cash
5	Globalization of regulatory environment	• Global regulation of the financial and the energy market • More cooperation between governments
6	Technology and Innovation	• Information technology plays a key role in globalization • Probability of groundbreaking innovations will rise
7	Scarcity of resources	• Energy supply and demand is the core problem for economic growth • Oil prices are on the rise again • Rising demand of emerging countries • Reduced food supply

Table 3: The top seven GETs of the 21st century

2.4.1 Collapsing Birthrate

The decline of birthrates is a phenomenon that has several implications for existing economies like the U.S., Japan, as well as, Europe, concerning the labor situation for companies, the healthcare system of a country, and the productivity of a nation. The effect will lead to less productivity, which will cause a drop of the economic status and raise the costs for healthcare.[29] Hence, the collapsing birthrate only affects established economies. The underdeveloped economies, but also emerging economies like India still grow in size, which directly implicates a rise in the world population.

"In fact, Japan and all of [...] Europe [...] are drifting toward a collective national suicide by the end of the 21st century. Even in Western and Northern Europe the birthrates are down to 1.5 and falling."[30] Even if birthrates in the developed world would develop better, it would take twenty years or so before these new babies would reach the age at which they join the labor force,[31] says Peter Drucker.

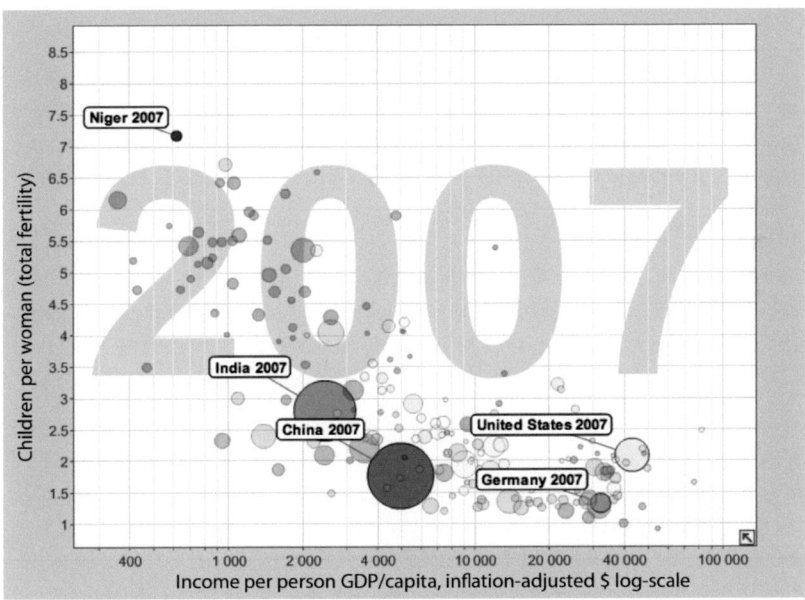

(Own creation, made with the gapminder software)

Figure 1: Total fertility and living standard by GDP / capita[32]

---
[29] Cf. Karalay (2005), p. 226
[30] Cf. Drucker (2007), p. 37
[31] Cf. Drucker (2007), p. 38
[32] Gapminder (2010)

The above figure, visualizes that in advanced economies like the U.S. and Germany women just tend to get between one or two children on the average per year. It is also depicted that in states like the Niger, one of the poorest countries in the world, women give birth to seven or more children. The economist introduced the metaphor replacement of fertility, which means, "... [In the established economies] half of humanity will be having enough children to replace itself"[33], because higher living standards, better communications and more education makes people rely on markets and public services, instead of oneself and family.[34]

To avoid a total collapse of the economic force, nations have to pursue the following policy. To ensure that the GDP remains on a stable level, companies need to acquire as much high-qualified personal from abroad as possible. Domestic companies need to beat the competition on the international job market with the help of the government, by paying higher wages than the competition, and by offering most attractive conditions for the families of the experts. Another way to raise the productive output of a nation, as elaborated in 1.4.1., is to reduce the unemployment rate.

To remain a stable GNP, national companies may invest in business overseas, to get the most profitable conditions for production, due to lower labor costs. This implies that companies and governments work closely together on the international platform to strengthen their investment relations.

2.4.2 Climate Change

More than ever, global environmental responsibility is the most important aspect concerning sustainable development of the ecology. Two terms from the corporate dictionary reflect this issue: responsibility and sustainability. Without a functional ecological environment, there will be even bigger problems like natural disasters.

Today, developed economies, as well as, emerging economies like China and India, are the largest causers of carbon emission, or the biggest polluters. Their job in the next decades has to be to reduce as much carbon emissions as possible to ensure sustainability and to protect the environment. The bottom line is that markets are not immune from the challenges of climate change. To illustrate the problem of the carbon dioxide emissions, the following figure illustrates the development of carbon dioxide emission by comparing the emission in relation to countries over time.

---

[33] Cf. The Economist (2009 c), p. 29
[34] Cf. The Economist (2009 c), p. 30

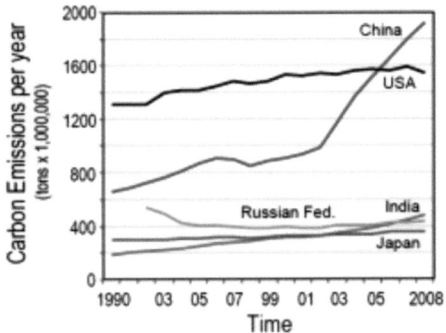

(Based on Global Carbon Consortium)

Figure 2:Global Carbon Emission[35]

Comparing sustainability of nation delivers further insights. In 2008, China already overtook the U.S. in the production of carbon dioxide concerning fossil fuel emissions.[36] In 2030, three-quarters of the global increase in CO_2 levels is expected to come from China and India.[37] Therefore, these economies need to be integrated into the process of carbon reduction. The European Commission claims that fossil fuels like oil, gas, and coal account for up to 80% of the EU's current energy supply. More than 50% is imported from outside the E.U.[38]

The requirement is that a significant reduction of carbon emissions up to 50% globally, and between 60-80% in developed countries by 2050, is needed.[39] There is a strong scientific and political consensus that a significant reduction of carbon emissions is required to limit the worst extremes of climate change. The political interplay in the past years hindered the reduction those emissions. Especially the ratification of the Kyoto protocol, which expires at the end of 2012, was a big problem, due to misinterpretations of governments and political blindness.

A large science group claims that carbon emissions are the key driver of temperature rise. Since the industrialization played the key role in development of nations and societies, the temperature rose constantly from the beginning of the 20th until today, which is depicted in the figure below. In the same breath, the sea level rose about 25 centimeters.[40]

---

[35] Cf. Global Carbon Project (2009), p. 8
[36] Cf. Global Carbon Project (2009), p. 8
[37] Cf. Ernst&Young (2009), p. 10
[38] Cf. European Energy Comission (2009), p. 10
[39] Cf. Ernst&Young (2009), p. 10
[40] Cf. IPCC (2007), pp. 420

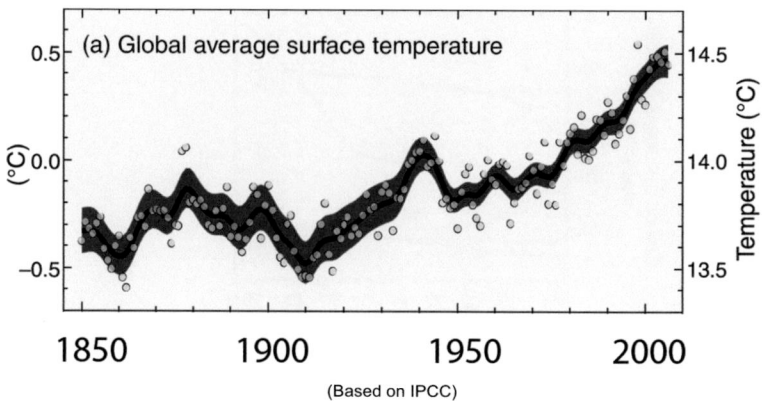

(Based on IPCC)

Figure 3: Development of the global surface temperature[41]

In advance of the United Nations climate change conference in December 2009 in Copenhagen (COP15), president Connie Heegaard said that if the world fails to deliver a political agreement it will be "the whole global democratic system not being able to deliver results in one of the defining challenges of our century".[42] Therefore, the complications that arise out of this global economic trend can only be solved if governments and nations agree on a global level to develop sustainable solutions and to apply these solutions on their domestic markets. From the macroeconomic point of view, this is a typical prisoner's dilemma, which can only be solved by political agreements.[43]

As it could have been expected, during the Copenhagen Summit that agreement was not achieved. Indeed, it showed that especially the emerging economies would not provide the reduction, because they strive for a better for a better living standard.[44]

In detail, two results have been achieved at the conference. First, politicians agreed on short-term funding for projects in developing country of $30 billion, which may aspire to a $100 billion budget a year for mitigation and adaptation from 2020 onwards. Second, the idea of holding global warming to no more than 2°C has been discussed. However, there have been no direct agreements or contracts. Concerning the achievements, the summit can be perceived as a failure.

---

[41] Cf. Global Warming (2010)
[42] Cf. United Nations (2009)
[43] Cf. The Economist (2009 b), p.4
[44] Cf. The Economist (2009 d)

2.4.3   Powershift from developed economies to emerging economies

With the words of Supachai Panitchpakdi, Secretary-General of UNCTAD: "In addition to private capital flows, many developing countries depend on foreign aid to support investment ... [and] lack the financial resources to successfully compete with the stimulus [of] emerging economies, which now amount to more than $5 trillion".[45] Furthermore, El-Erian states: "The growth strategies adopted by several emerging economies have resulted in a rapid increase in their share of the world trade". Indeed, there is a strong consensus among experts that the economic power will shift from developed to emerging economies. The steady progress of the emerging economies capturing global market share is depicted in the following figure.[46]

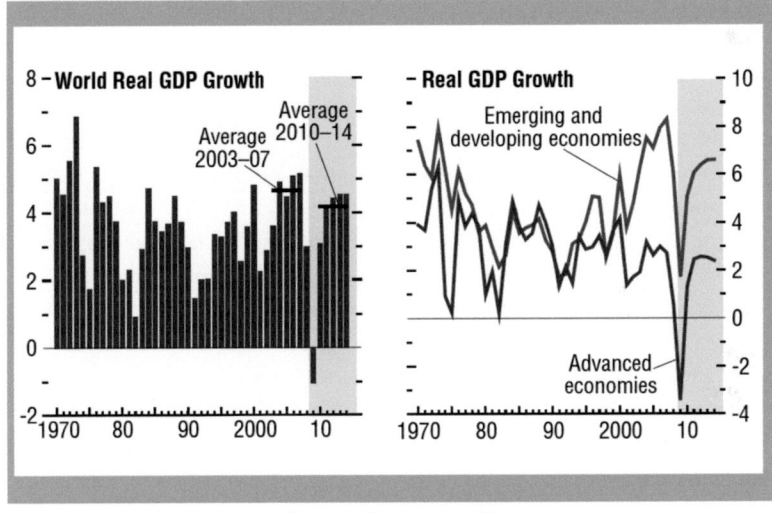

(Own creation, based on IMF)

Figure 4: World Real GDP Growth[47]

According to the real GDP forecast of the IMF, advanced economies are projected to expand sluggishly through much of 2010, with unemployment continuing to rise until later in the year. The annual growth in 2010 is projected to be about 1.25 percent, following a contraction of 3.50 percent in 2009.[48] In emerging economies, real GDP growth is forecast to reach almost 6.5 percent in 2010. Compared to 2009 this is an increase of almost 5 percent. The driving forces for this

---

[45] Cf. United Nations (2009 a)
[46] Cf. International Monetary Fund (2009), p.4
[47] Cf. International Monetary Fund (2009), p.6
[48] Cf. International Monetary Fund (2009), p.9

development come from China, India, and a number of other emerging Asian economies. Other emerging economies are staging modest recoveries, supported by policy stimulus and improving global trade and financial conditions.[49]

It must be stated here, that beside the economic tendencies, there is also a cultural change involved in the power shift. Especially MNCs need to be aware of these economies to ensure a sustainable growth of their business. From the marketing point of view, their products need to meet the requirements of new customers. In summary, the new players on the financial and economical market already have a huge influence, and will gain an even stronger position in the future.

2.4.4   Changing financial landscape

Due to the globalization, today's international financial markets are linked and depend on each other. The best prove is the breakdown of established financial markets after the U.S. subprime crisis, which had an impact to the global investment world and led to a global recession. In 2009, economic growth has turned positive again, "... as wide-ranging public intervention has supported demand and lowered uncertainty and systemic risk in financial markets".[50] Of special interest is that emerging markets revitalized from the financial crash very fast. In an article called "An astonishing rebound" the Economist postulated that the real GDP of the four emerging Asian economies (China, Indonesia, South Korea, and Singapore) grew by an annualized rate of 10%,[51] due to several effects. First, simply because the national demand for manufactured products e.g. cars rose again. Second, regions export exacerbated by the freezing up of global financial trade in 2008 increased, as well as, third, the domestic spending of money.[52]

Concerning the credit crunch and recovery, this development has also two side effects. Especially established economies will suffer from this development, as the economic growth will slow down after the recession. Hence, the time of recovery will be prolonged, because new capital is harder to assess. Emerging economies will only suffer temporary, because they hold enough capital, which will help them in their growth process. Therefore, these economies will lead the world through the crisis. To perceive the impact of the credit crunch, above figure illustrates decline of the S&P 500 index from its peak during the sub prime crisis, or credit crunch, in comparison to other market crashes.

---

[49] Cf. International Monetary Fund (2009), p. 51
[50] Cf. International Monetary Fund (2009), p. XIV
[51] Cf. Economist (2009 e), p.15
[52] Cf. Economist (2009 e), p.19

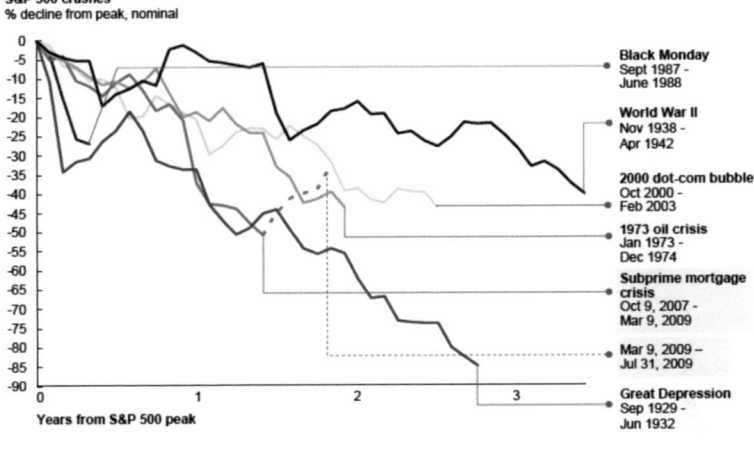

(Based on MCKinsey)

Figure 5: Impact of the crisis[53]

In a wider sense, the financial landscape has changed completely and new players play a dominant role on the global financial market. Especially, player from the emerging economies gained strong influence on the international level. To illustrate this global economic trend, the outward foreign direct investment indicator, which includes the three components equity capital, reinvested earnings, and intra-company loans, is used to show in what manner an economy invests into another economy. In numbers, worlds foreign direct investments where about $ 1.8 trillion in 2008 in total shares and cash flows,[54] and foreign investors owning over 25% of global equities. As the researchers of Ernst&Young found out that, the outcome is "that emerging markets are now the net providers of capital flows, financing the large current account deficits of the developed countries, in particular the U.S."[55]

In a narrower sense, four new kinds of brokers, the so-called power brokers are now the key players on the international financial market. These are the (a) petrodollar investors, (b) Asian central banks, which often use sovereign wealth funds as investment vehicles, (c) hedge funds, and (d) private equity investors.[56] A report published by McKinsey Global Institute illustrates the enormous potential and the growing assets of these players, which are depicted below.

---

[53] Cf. McKinsey (2009), p. 10
[54] Cf. United Nations (2009 b), p. 2
[55] Cf. Enrst&Young (2009), p.4
[56] Cf. McKinsey (2007), p.9

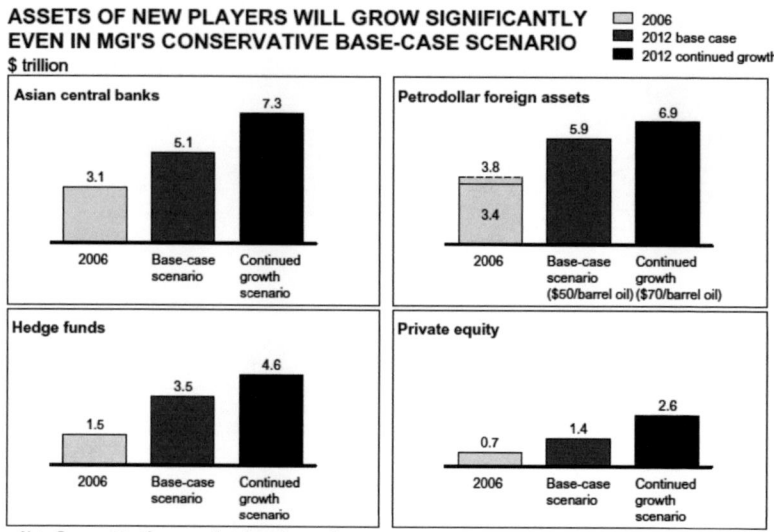

(Based on MCKinsey)

Figure 6: The asset forecast of the power investors[57]

Their asset volume was roughly about $8.47 tn in 2006 and their volume in 2012 is estimated to be about $19.4 tn in 2012, which is another prove that the influence of these players grows stronger.

Even though, the growth of these players is mutually reinforcing. On the one hand, petrodollar investors and Asian central banks are both providing huge capital flows on a regular basis, but also in the gray area between government and private. On the other hand, Hedge funds and private equity push the risk-return frontier in new directions.[58] In conclusion, the illustrated new players will dominate the financial markets in the 21st century. In this regard, corporations have to incorporate this influence into their business planning, especially when it comes to investment decision.

---

[57] Cf. Mc Kinsey (2007), p. 26
[58] Cf. McKinsey (2007), p.9

2.4.5 Globalization of regulatory environment

A significant urgency that arises from the global financial crisis is the need for a more robust and globally constant regulation, primarily for the financial market, but also other sectors like food and energy. With the words of Nobel price winner Joseph Stieglitz: "Unless we have an adequate regulatory system—regulations and a regulatory structure that ensures their implementation—we are bound to have another crisis."[59] Finding the right model is only one significant challenge; the other is to reach an agreement on the global level, or with the words of Lipschutz: "As a rule, the variation is less a matter of existing legislation than enforcement of these laws".[60]

Tension lays in-between companies that strive for profits on the global market, as well as, in-between governments, which tend to implement protective measures like trade barriers or tariffs to protect their domestic market. Thus, reaching a consensus on an international level is one side of the coin. Monitoring and enforcing these rules is the other. In this sense, regulation can be defined as "the organization and control of economic, political, and social activities by means of making, implementing, monitoring, and enforcing of rules".[61]

The question that arises out of this context is if existing organizations like the like the United Nations, the G8, or the G20 have the power for enforcement, or if there is the need to establish a new control organization. The ideal model of global regulation, also described as global governance, needs changes on two dimensions. National political responsibility should shift to a global level and at the same time, national economical problems should be delegated to those supranational institutions.[62] However, giving up national control to achieve a better collaboration between nations is a difficult task. The European Union is still the only an example, where international agreements have been established to regulate legislation and trade in-between European countries. Nevertheless, during the crisis in 2009, the rapid actions of policy makers worldwide helped to avoid a total dry out of the liquidity. With the words of Dominique Strauss-Kahn, president of the IMF: "In the financial sector, enhanced international co-operation is needed to overcome possibly divergent national interests and so achieve meaningful reform in 2010."[63]

---

[59] Cf. The Big Picture (2008)
[60] Cf. Lipschutz(2005), p.15
[61] Cf. Mattli (2009), p.1
[62] Cf. Mattli (2009), p.242
[63] Cf. Economist (2009 ff), p.23

2.4.6 Technology and Innovation

It is proven throughout the history of industrialization that technology plays a key role in the development of the human race. For example, the inventions of the steam machine, the automobile, the telephone, the computer, or the Internet have changed business processes and the way on how people interact with each other. Those groundbreaking inventions came out of nowhere, like a black swan, and revolutionized the status quo of the world in its time. Even though, those paradigm changes also had an enormous economical impact. The problem with such technologies is to perceive the possibilities that arise out of the innovation. This leads to the fact that the right innovation is a global economic trendsetter by itself, and the early adopters of this technology innovation will always be a winner in global competition.[64]

This trend should now be illustrated by discussitial of information technology. ial of information technology. Peter Drucker's example of the New Information Revolution delivers evidence that technological radically changes "the MEANING of information ... not in technology, machinery, techniques..., but in concepts"[65]. Some years later Jack Walsh postulated that the Internet is "the single most important event in the U.S. economy since the Industrial Revolution".[66] From the scientific point of view, the Internet enables technologist from different research sites to interact through the Internet for the exchange of knowledge and information. The phrase the transformative power of the Internet is a decent description of this phenomenon.[67] Even though, it must be stated here that some sectors of the economy will benefit more than others. Information driven industries are the winners, such as finance services, entertainment, or high technology.[68] This leads to the hypothesis that the probability of groundbreaking innovations will rise in the future, due to an even higher productivity of science and a faster rate of innovation. A prove to this hypothesis is the amount of scientific papers that are submitted at big international conferences. For example, At this year's international conference for Computer and Industrial Engineering, CIE, over 50 nations have participated, 700 papers have been submitted, of which 337 articles have been published by the IEEE.[69] In conclusion, information technology will be the key driver in science and technology of the 21st century.

---

[64] Cf. Welfens (1999), p. 130
[65] Cf. Drucker, p. 82
[66] Cf. Price (2000), p.45
[67] Cf. Dess (2007), p. 263
[68] Cf. Dess (2007), p.263
[69] Cf. IEE (2009)

2.4.7 Scarcity of resources

Energy supply and demand is one of the major challenges of tomorrow for nations, governments, and institutions, as it is the center of global economics, geopolitics, war, fiscal policy, and the battle between growth and stability.[70] Especially the supply of energy will become one of the biggest problems, because the trend is that resources will be even scarcer in the near future, due to the fact the world population is on the rise, and emerging countries strive for more wealth. This leads automatically to an increase in prices and to a reduced capacity of energy resources. As an example, the Economist stated in an article that global oil demand would rise again in 2010, but slowly, reaching for a price goal of $100 per barrel, until the end of the year.[71]

Indeed, oil plays the most important role in meeting the future energy demand for several reasons. First, oil is important for the socio-economic development of nations, because it is directly connected with transportation costs. Second, oil price volatility renders all the more difficult the interpretation of price signals, whether they are an indication of structural change or a reflection of temporary phenomena, and thereby affecting the ability to support longer-term market stability.[72] Therefore, the given dynamic of oil markets should be regulated, a support of fair and stable prices is required, and a sustainability of supply, to ensure demand. Consequently, two main problems arise out of the context. First, there is a lack in regulating the oil production and controlling its trade. The OPEC, which stands for Organization of the Petroleum Exporting Countries, founded in 1960, tries to regulate the production volumes, or supply quotas, and thereby the development of the oil price.[73] Even thought that the OPEC controls over 40% of the world's oil production, it has lost its influence over the years, as oil producing nations start to offer oil outside of the OPEC.[74] Yet, the only institution that acts as a global policy advisor is the International Energy Agency (IEA), which has been established after the oil crisis in 1974.[75] Besides oil and gas, renewable energy is also in the focus of the agency. However, they are not powerful enough to dictate prices. In general, markets lack of effective control mechanisms, because oil prices are often high through speculations of investors on trading futures of Brent and WTI.[76]

---

[70] Cf. Ernst&Young (2009), p. 8
[71] Cf. The Economist (2009 f), p. 34
[72] Cf. Opec (2009), p. 6
[73] Cf. Investorword (2010)
[74] Cf. Investor Verlag (2008)
[75] Cf. International Energy Agency (2009)
[76] Cf. Hoffmann (2010)

Second, there is the problem of peak oil. The term describes the point in time where a limit in the oil delivery volume for a single oilfield or an oil region, has been reached.[77] This point is the turning point for cheap oil-based energy, which has been the economic engine of the past, postulates to Colin Campbell founder of the Association for the Study of Peak Oil&Gas (ASPO). His argument is that banks did not recognize this logical interconnection, and their reaction to print money under the Keynesian principle is not the right approach to restore past prosperity, because this would again stimulate the demand for oil and lead to further price shocks and recessions.[78]

Economic growth does not depend on the total capacity of oil, but on the actual capacity, which regulates the development of the prices. As a sidenote, the remaining total capacity of oil is estimated to remain for 20 until 50 years.[79] Status quo is that 28 billion barrels a year support a world population on 6.7 bn people today. Nevertheless, by 2050, the supply of oil cannot support less than half the number of people in their present way of life.[80] Especially with the rising demand on energy by emerging economies, this limit can be reached even faster. E.g., the accumulated need of cars by these economies is gigantic. Today, there are seven cars per thousand inhabitants in India and eight in china. Compared to Germany there are 546 cars per inhabitant.[81] Even if this density doubles in the next years, the demand for steals, aluminum, and oil will explode.

Besides the direct problem involved with scarcity of oil, is the interconnection with food crops. Concerning energy supply, biofuels are competing with food crops, which is a prisoner's dilemma. On the one hand, food demand is still rising because of changing appetites and rising incomes in emerging markets. On the other hand, big oil companies perceive biofuel as an answer to the oil problem.[82]

2.5   Impact to corporations

Without a doubt, the transformational power of GETs will drive industries and markets to a new secular destination. Due to this, corporations need to adapt existing business processes, strategic planning, and the corporate culture, to meet the requirements of the new scenario. This is valid for multinational companies (MNCs), but also small and medium type enterprises (SMEs). In order to identify the actual impact to corporations, the overall business situation needs to be incorporated. In other words, the value chain, and the interdepencies between

---

[77] Cf. PeakOil (2010)
[78] Cf. Campbell (2009)
[79] Cf. PeakOil (2009)
[80] Cf. Campbell (2009)
[81] Cf. Buchholtz (2006)
[82] Cf. The Economist (2009 g), p. 13

markets and corporations need to be deconstructed.[83] This includes the
stakeholders, the shareholders, primary activities, secondary activities, as well as,
the overall business portfolio. To demonstrate this complexity, the relationship is
demonstrated in the figure below.

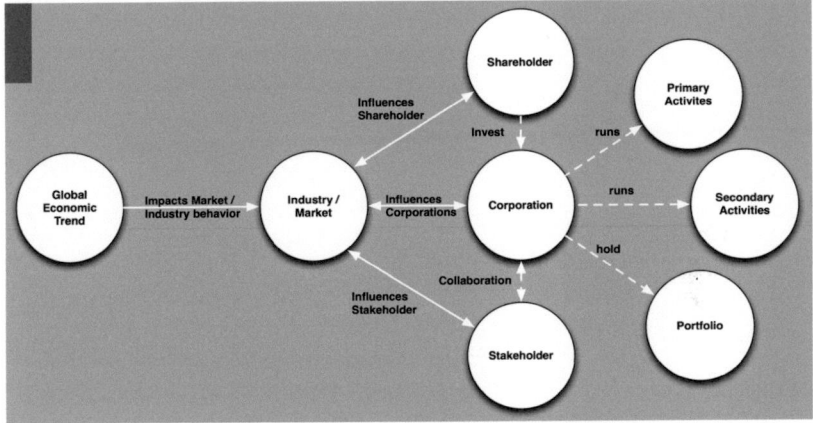

(Own creation, based on Boston Consulting Group)

Figure 7: The impact to corporations[84]

Thereby, management needs to clearly identify the parts that are influenced
mostly by a certain trend; afterwards a strategy should be developed. As depicted
a corporation is always embedded in a complex interplay.

Even though, the position of shareholders and stakeholders is also influenced by
the GET, and the action of these partner can be influenced, but not controlled
directly by the corporation. Furthermore, some activities within the primary
activities, which include all the upstream and downstream processes, may involve
some corporation with external shareholders. Hence, the corporation has to find a
methodology to access the direct and indirect impact of a GET to the business.
Moreover, strategy has to incorporate these impacts, which manifest in internal
and external threats to the business. Last but not least, due to the global
interconnection between markets, which is especially true for the financial and the
energy market, GETs are interdependent and they work at the same time on the
route to a new secular destination, which may become a new form of equilibrium.

---

[83] Cf. Boston Consulting Group (2006), p. 105
[84] Cf. Boston Consulting Group (2006), pp.112

3   Corporate Development

The core of the Corporate Development (CD) evaluation is the GET Assessment Framework that delivers the methodology on how to tackle the challenges that arise out of the analysis of global economic trends. To integrate this framework into the strategic planning process, this chapter provides a holistic view on the concept of CD. Therefore, the analysis contains the principles of corporate development, which includes strategic planning, portfolio management, value based management, risk management, and change management.

3.1   Definition of Corporate Development

Corporate Development can be defined as the management of the corporate portfolio with the toolsets of strategic management.[85] Corporate Strategy (CS) is at the heart of corporate development. It has many facets, and each approach to the topic has its own concepts and intellectual pedigree.[86] In simple terms, it concerns the long-term survival and growth of business organizations,[87] by emphasizing the overall direction in the wider, and in the narrower sense.

For MNCs, the wider sense is about the question in which businesses the company should invest. In contrast, the narrower sense refines the business analysis, by asking in what countries/markets is the enterprise in, and in what countries/markets it should be in.[88] Therefore, CD concentrates on CS, which is the top level strategy of the company, concerned with the overall scope of an organization and how value is added to the organization.[89] The main target for Corporate Development is to raise the value of the corporation.[90]

Below the top level of strategy, there are two more mutually exclusive levels of strategy, business level-strategy, and operational-level strategy, which have to be inline with the top-level strategy so that the company can gain competitive advantage.[91] Hence, CS lays the foundation for strategic planning process in MNCs, and builds the connective link between corporate strategy, or the business targets, and the operational (functional) management. Therefore, it is about bridging the gap, by identifying the constraints to the business targets and to juxtapose them to existing company assets and business processes. In this case, CS can be perceived as a bridge over the divide.

---

[85] Cf. Grant (2005), p. 477
[86] Cf. Whittington (2001), p. 9
[87] Cf. Sutton (1980), p.1
[88] Cf. Robin (1996), p. 176
[89] Cf. Whittington (2001), p.7
[90] Cf. Colley (), pp. 6
[91] Cf. Porter (1998), p. 39

3.2   Strategic planning process

Multinational companies handle strategic business planning as a process that incorporates all management levels within a company. These levels can be visualized, when a corporation is sliced into lean, and mean strategic business units (SBUs) that summarize a specific product, or a specific production process, as depicted below.

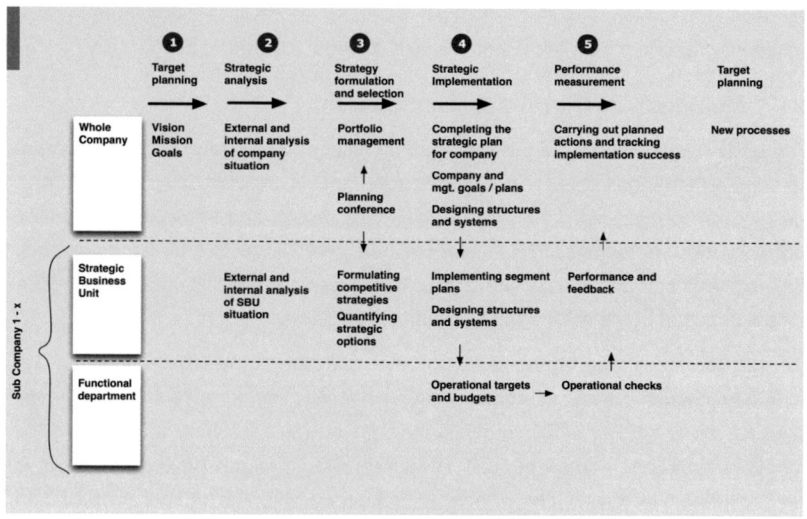

(own creation, based on Roland Berger)

Figure 8: Strategic Planning Process[92]

Each of the specific SBU may be embedded into its own sub company, as depicted above. This is true for corporations that are organized as a holding structure. Functional departments are led by an individual management, which controls and organizes the actual working processes and implements the strategy. The model inherits five process steps, which are repeated after completion. As an outcome, Corporate Strategy should be refined and implemented throughout the organization to ensure that success potentials, such as a desired target market position, competitive advantage[93] in the market, and competitive advantage in resources is ensured.[94] This process of management planning, also called total business strategy,[95] is a common procedure along MNCs, and may only differ by its business configuration.

---

[92] Cf. Roland Berger (2010)
[93] Cf. Porter (1998), p. 131
[94] Cf. Grüning (2008), p. 32
[95] Cf. Smit (2007), p 53

3.2.1 Target Planning

Target planning begins with the decision-making of the management board and the supervisory board, who define the annual or quarterly business goals, concerning the expectations of the shareholders and the stakeholders. The aim of the target planning is to define strategic targets for the corporate value of the company, to meet the shareholder and stakeholder expectations of the corporation.[96]

The timeframe of reporting is related to how the company reports its business achievement to the public. In turbulent times, the timeframe is even shorter, because the business goals need to be refined to reflect the actual business position. Another crucial element concerning GETs is shareholder value expectation versus economic growth. Because economic growth is stagnating, the management of the company needs to ensure that shareholders get the right view on the company potential before they do their investments. In summary, these normative goals are the target goals for operational business. The job of CD is to translate these goals into tasks for the SBUs.

3.2.2 Strategic Analysis

Identification of the as-is situation is the beginning of the business planning process, and is the core of CD. To perceive the status quo means that the CD unit needs to corporate with the management of the SBUs within the company for the evaluation. The business position is reflected internally and externally, due to a SWOT analysis.[97] As depicted below, the internal strength and weaknesses are juxtaposed against external threats and weaknesses.

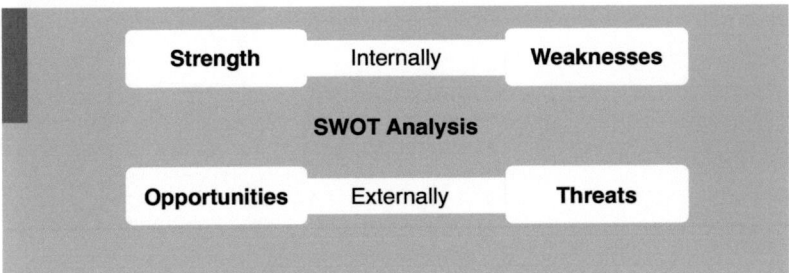

(Own creation)

Figure 9: SWOT Analysis

---

[96] Cf. von Düsterlho (2003), p. 163
[97] Cf. Thompson (2008), p. 97

The SWOT analysis should comprise further toolsets that are used to analyze the external and the internal position of the company. For example, five forces or PEST(el) analysis. In short, the external analysis identifies opportunities and threats in the economical environment, by recognizing the market size and business position, as well as, estimate the possible market for the products or services.[98] The internal analysis erodes the strength and weaknesses of the company. This position is clarified by estimating the actual financial situation, vis-à-vis, and the value configuration.

Concerning GETs, this approach must include verification of possible threats that arise from GETs. The CD unit then needs to analyze a GET in regard to urgency. Based on this decision, change management projects can be planned beforehand, to establish countermeasures against possible threats and weaknesses that can occur in the future. This approach is refined within the chapter of change management. To prove the theoretical foundation, the case study of this paper shows how a company that operates in the chemical industry evaluates threats.

3.2.3   Strategy formulation and selection

After the as-is situation is clarified, the strategy formulation and selection is performed. Regarding the actual business situation, the management can choose between different strategies.

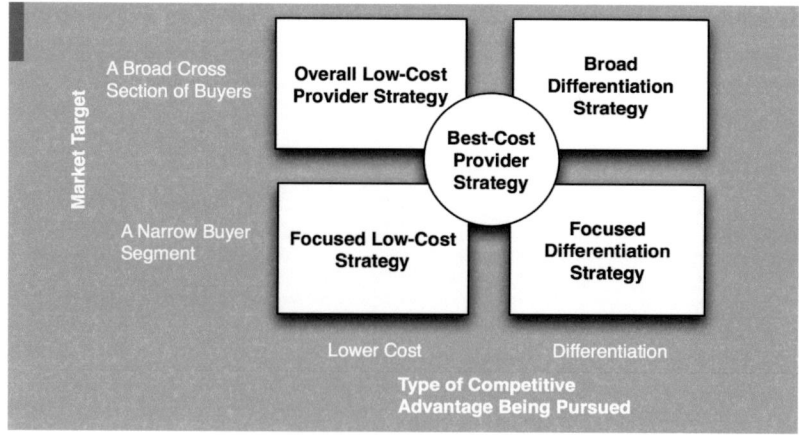

(Own creation)

Figure 10: Five generic strategies[99]

---

[98] Cf. Thompson (2008), p. 108
[99] Cf. Thompson (2008), p. 134

Depicted above, these strategies are also referred as the five generic strategies.[100] If strategies for the overall business, and the SBUs are clarified, the setup of the Portfolio needs to be verified to ensure the validity of the strategies, because strategies may differ across the business units. To clarify the strategy and to justify its means, the CD-unit needs to works together with the management the SBUs to the quantity of measures.

As a hypothesis about GETs, the forces of GETs also influence the competitive environment. Therefore, the analysis of the competitive environment needs to be reflected to this influence, to avoid a misconception of the strategy. Then the strategy is formulated, and carried out to the functional or operational management division within the SBU.

3.2.4 Strategic implementation

After the strategic implementation is clarified, the strategy is implemented within the company. In this time, the overall approach is juxtaposed to the actual business goals, and the strategic roadmap is completed. At this stage, plans are turned into action assignments in a manner that accomplishes the plan's stated objectives.[101] The stage can be defined as the communication, interpretation, and enactment of strategic plans.[102] In other words, overall business targets of the corporation are fine tuned and adjusted to the value configuration of the SBU. This encompasses the designing of systems and structures. Especially changes in the competitive environment necessitate adjustments to the organizational structure.[103]

3.2.5 Performance measurement

After the strategy has been implemented in the value creation process, the performance of the strategy needs to be measured in order to find out if it actually works. If not, then the strategy needs to be adopted. Measurement of the progress is based on the defined business goals, as well as, on key performance indicators (KPIs), which vary according to the business process, and to the strategic level within the organization. An overview of the most important value based indictors is given in chapter 3.4.2.

On the strategic level of the department, key performance indicators are related to the production and service processes. For example, a KPI can be lead time-to-

---

[100] Cf. Thompson (2008), p. 134
[101] Cf. Smit (2007), p.15
[102] Cf. Smit (2007), p.16
[103] Cf. Smit (2007), p. 17

market,[104] which measures the time from innovation to the final sale of a product to a customer. The strategic level of the SBU encompasses indicators that measure the performance of the inherited functional units. In this case, a KPI can be gained revenue, and of course, return on invest (ROI). It is also possible to estimate the attractiveness of a certain SBU with a technique called SBU assessment,[105] by reflecting the individual performance to the industry and the group performance.

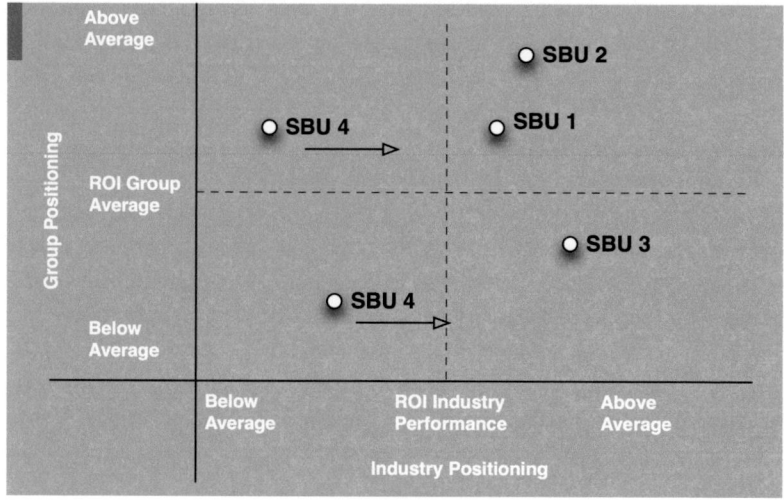

(Own creation)

Figure 11: SBU assesment

As depicted above, the concept of SBU assessment juxtaposes the actual as-is performance to the will-be performance that has been defined through the strategic assessment of the CD unit. With this technique, it is possible to determine the real performance of a SBU in comparison to a well-defined peer group. If a MNC is diversified in many industries, then the SBU assessment has to be done in relation to the performance of a certain industry. Concerning GETS, this framework is also perfect to analyze how a GET is affecting the development of a whole industry. In addition, the management of the company sees how the well a SBU is really performing. The overall performance of the strategy can be measured with the sum of the SBU individual KPIs results. It must be stated here that traditional accounting measures like ROI, or also unit costs per production,

---

[104] Cf. Locher (2008), p. xi
[105] Cf. Aswathappa (2008), p. 298

can give misleading signals for continuous improvement, innovation, and competence-building activities.[106]

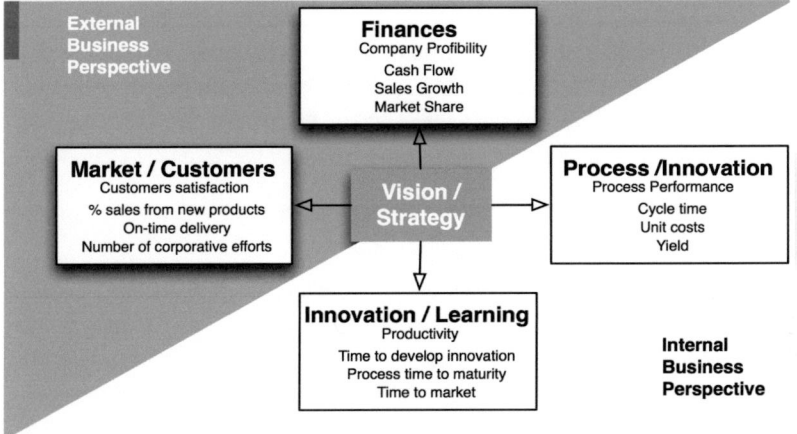

(Own creation, based on Smit)[107]
Figure 12: Balanced Scorecard

In this regard, these KPIs need to be enriched with conceptual frameworks such as the balanced scorecard approach of Kaplan and Norton, which is depicted above. This toolset enhances the business planning process by reflecting the corporate strategy to the actual business goals. As Kaplan stated: "a scorecard should not only be derived from the organization's strategy; it should also be transparent back to the strategy".[108] Therefore, this approach should be used to plan and to reflect the actual strategy to the business situation. By means of active evaluation, the business strategy can be refined to meet the desired business situation concerning the following aspects: Company profitability, customer satisfaction, process performance, and the ability to learn. To give an alternative, the five-dimension framework from the total quality management (TQM) approach can also be applied for the refinement process.[109] In summary, the measurement of performance needs to incorporate a total view on the strategy. This can be achieved by implementing value performance indicators and by enhancing the overall process by applying framework like business scorecard.

---

[106] Cf. Verweire (2004), p. 37
[107] Cf. Smit (2005), p.239
[108] Cf. Kaplan (1996), p. 148
[109] Cf. Smith (2005), p.92

3.3   Value-based Management

Value in the corporate dictionary is defined as the relationship between a return that is generated by business activities and resources that are consumed within the activity.[110] The previous chapter pointed several times at the measurement of strategic performance. This chapter now resolves these issues by introducing the methodologies of value management, which in relation to CD refers to enhancement of the value of the corporation, commonly known as the shareholder value.[111]

3.3.1   Concept of value-based management

In short, value management focuses on the management of the corporate value with the tools of strategic management, to meet the expectation of the shareholders and stakeholders of the corporation.[112] The target planning and strategic analysis phase of the strategy planning process implies the enhancement of enterprise value, which is done through the process of measuring, controlling, and distribution.[113]

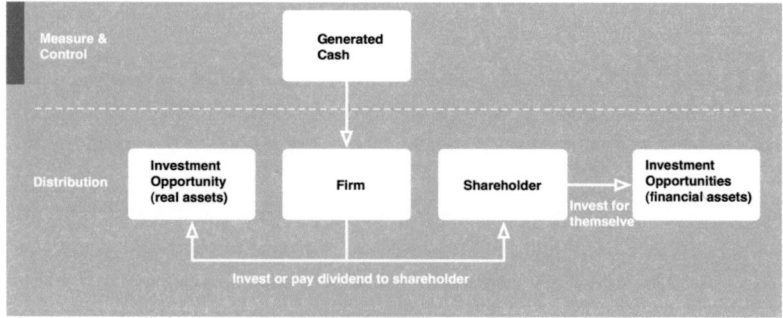

(Own creation, based on Myers)

Figure 13: Investment decision[114]

As depicted above, the layer measuring and control relates to how much value, shown as generated cash, is created at a time. Distribution involves the decision-making whether to re-invest in new business opportunities, or to pay out dividends to shareholder. The opportunity cost of reinvesting is the expected rate of return that shareholders could have obtained by financial assets.[115]

---

[110] Cf. Scarlett (2001), p. v
[111] Cf. Hammerschmidt (2006), p.90
[112] Cf. Schweikart (2006), p. 3
[113] Cf. Schweikart (2006), p. 15
[114] Cf. Brealey (2003), p. 92
[115] Cf. Brealey (2003), p.92

3.3.2   Value based performance indicators

Value based performance indicators help to identify the actual value added, or the value proposition, and to reflect it to the capital base. They are the basis to successful business planning.[116] To pinpoint their importance, the approach starts with the balance sheet, which is the foundation concerning performance measuring, as depicted below.

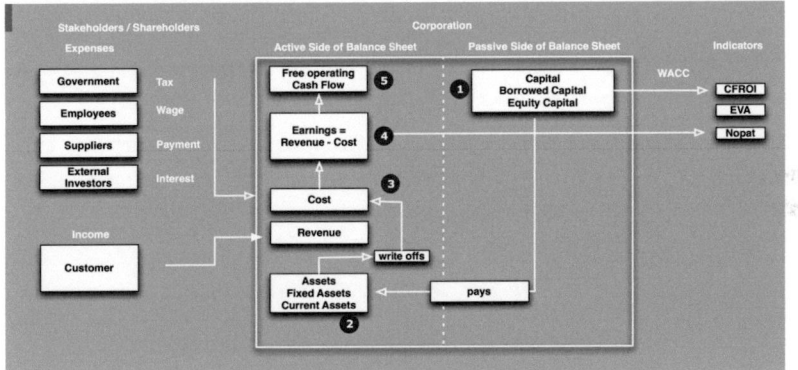

(Own creation, based on Dresdner model)[117]

Figure 14: Active and passive side of the balance sheet

The starting point of the analysis is capital, which is equity and borrowed (debt) capital, represented as (1). Based on this capital, assets are financed (2); these investments consist of investment capital and working capital.[118] From the investments the depreciation and amortization of intangible assets, property, plant, equipments, and financial assets are paid (3). Expenses cover also the interests, taxes, payments, and wages. The difference between revenues, which is gained from sales and costs are the earnings (4). The effort and yield is the profit, which is commonly known as Net Operating Profit After Tax (NOPAT). NOPAT can also be calculated as the earnings before interest and taxes (EBIT) minus taxes. Once the NOPAT has been estimated it is not far to the cash flow, or free operating cash flow (FCF) of the company (5). Because, the NOPAT is calculated periodically, the net investments need to be integrated into the calculation to get the FCF. The depreciation needs to be added, capital expenditure and new working capital need to be subtracted.[119]

---

[116] Cf. von Düsterlho (2003), p. 163
[117] Cf. Schweikart (2006), p. 12
[118] Cf. Schweikart (2006), p.28
[119] Cf. Antil (2005), p. 19

Therefore, the FCF represents the actual money the company has earned and that is available for future investments. As a side note, this value is also used for several valuation methods. At this point it is also important to refer to the most famous shareholder valuation models such as the multiplier method, the discounted cash flow method (DCF), or the earned value added (EVA) method. The models are used to valuate companies, by estimating the future results of the business. The foundation to these methodologies are the risk adjusted weighted average costs of capital (WACC). This measure ads risk elements like risk premium and debt/equity mix to the valuation, to cover possible risks. However, it does not address all possible risks.[120]

This is a very important point regarding the analysis of GETs, which are only accessible on an intuitive risk analysis. As a rule, only the interest-bearing liabilities and the balance sheet equity (also: market capitalization) are used.[121]

To conclude the above analysis, there is a difference between value-based indicators based on cash flow and earnings. For successful business planning depends cash flow based indicators more important, because they are closer related to the shareholders. To conclude the analysis, the following figure gives an overview of earnings and cash flow based indicators.

Value-orientated KPIs		
Basis	Earnings	Cash Flow
Value added	Excess profit	Excess Cash flow
Absolute	Residual Earnings	Residual Cash Flow
	EVA	CVA
	EP	SVA
	GWB	
Realtive	Profitability figures	
	ROI	CFROI
	ROC	SVR
	RONA	
	ROCE	
Increase in value	Earnings per capital unit	

(Own creation, based on Töpfer)

Figure 15: Value based indicators[122]

---

[120] Cf. Wyman (2007), p. 4
[121] Cf. Wiehle (2007), p.229
[122] Cf. Schweikart (2006), p.31

3.4   Portfolio Management

Based on the distinction between financial and business portfolios, the following paragraph describes the differences and the commonalities among those types of portfolios, and illustrates the main approaches and methodologies, which are used to manage portfolios concerning GETs.

3.4.1   Concept of a Portfolio

To emphasize the importance of portfolio management, it is important to distinguish between two definitions of portfolios, most commonly used in the corporate world. These are the financial and the business portfolio. In both cases, a portfolio can be perceived as a simultaneous view on assets, to measure the configuration, or the status quo of the actual composition. Both portfolios are mutually linked with each other, but the approaches of management differ. The question is therefore, what is the difference between the portfolios and what is their core intention. According to Spreemann, a financial portfolio is a conceptual sum of capital assets by a person, a household, or an institution, in order to visualize the actual financial value of the overall assets, to estimate returns, as well as, to expose the returns to possible risks.[123] In contrast to a financial portfolio, a business portfolio is the logical total of the overall sub businesses. An element of the total is the strategic business unit (SBU), which can be perceived as a company division, a product line within a division, or sometimes just a single product or brand.[124] Concerning this, the distinction is made based on revenues and strategy.[125]

3.4.2   Corporate Portfolio Management

In times of secular transformations, aligning the right information to successfully plan and to manage a corporate portfolio is challenging to corporate managers, especially when addressing resource (capital allocation) and investment decisions.[126] Management needs to incorporate both, the quantitative (financial) aspects, and the qualitative (business) aspects, to successfully manage a corporate portfolio, especially when coping with uncertainty and the forces of GETs. To illustrate the difference between these approaches, the following figure gives and overview of common approaches, which are used within corporate development.

---

[123] Cf. Spreemann (2006), p. 8
[124] Cf. Kottler (2002), p. 139
[125] Cf. Scheuss (2007), p. 82
[126] Cf. Wyman (2007), p. 2

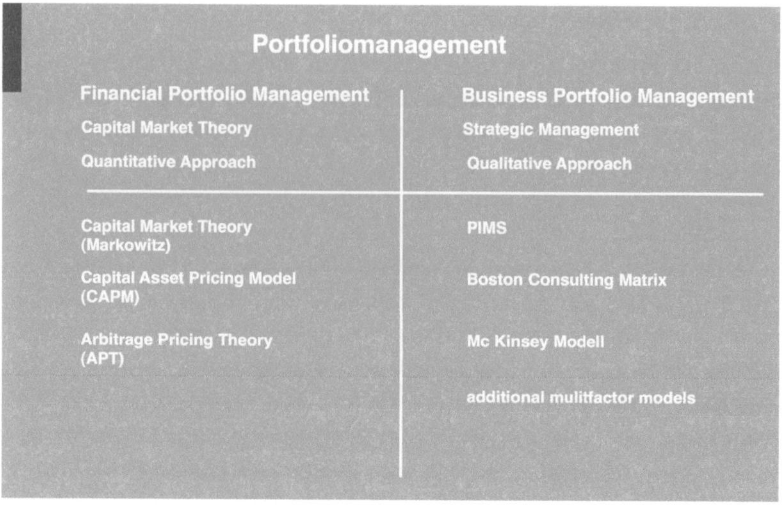

Portfoliomanagement

Financial Portfolio Management	Business Portfolio Management
Capital Market Theory	Strategic Management
Quantitative Approach	Qualitative Approach
Capital Market Theory (Markowitz)	PIMS
Capital Asset Pricing Model (CAPM)	Boston Consulting Matrix
Arbitrage Pricing Theory (APT)	Mc Kinsey Modell
	additional mulitfactor models

(Own creation, based on Weller)

Figure 16: Theory of Portfolio Management[127]

Strategic Portfolio Management is an essential condition of sustainable growth. Portfolio decisions must have a solid quantitative foundation and must be based on the principles of value-based management, which is also explained within this chapter. Value can only be gained, if a corporation is able to nurture the potentials of their business portfolio, and deploy their resources effectively, like physical assets, intangible assets, and capabilities, for example development skills.[128] To successfully manage a corporate portfolio and to create value, executives must increasingly balance investment opportunities against the capital that is available to finance them.[129] Hence, a robust approach that analyses each option's risk-return trade-off and reflects each option's overall impact on the existing portfolio has to be the foundation of investment decisions.[130]

Three strategic levers raise the value of a corporate portfolio, which are (a) portfolio optimization, (b) diversification, and (c) divestments of portfolio assets.[131] The tools that are introduced within this chapter help to determine the actual portfolio situation, and to develop a target portfolio. Latter sets the target for quantitative goals for value-based measures, and corporate strategy.

---

[127] Cf. Wellner (2003), p. 158
[128] Cf. Hahn (2005), p. 77
[129] Cf. Carlesi (2007), p.2
[130] Cf. Weyman (2007), p.2
[131] Cf. Boston Consulting Group, pp.268

3.4.3   Financial portfolio management

3.4.3.1 Modern Portfolio Theory

Modern financial portfolio theory is the one of the most important and influential economic theories about finance and investment, and was awarded in 1990 with the Nobel Prize for Economics. Before this theory, models only included a two-dimensional perspective on volatility and return characteristics of individual securities.[132] Markowitz incorporated a third dimension that evaluated the degree of diversification of a portfolio. He showed how exactly an investor can reduce the standard deviation of portfolio returns by choosing stocks that do not move exactly together.[133] Based on these concepts he worked out principles for the optimal construction of a portfolio, which is also perceived asset allocation. This model is the basis for further developments, like the model of Sharpe, and even more important the capital asset pricing model.[134] Companies that follow the diversification strategy are called conglomerates. In simple terms, this mathematical theory has several premises:[135]

- Investors are risk averse.

- They strive for maximum profit and minimal risk

- Securities are traded in efficient markets

- Risk is judged on the overall portfolio, rather than looking on individual assets. For every level of risk there is an optimal portfolio of assets that will have the highest expected returns

- An optimal portfolio has the highest expected returns.

The model is most interesting to broad diversified companies, also called conglomerates. Shareholders can choose to buy either a diversified portfolio of shares, or a share with a diversified portfolio.[136] Mathematically, the core of Markowitz theory is the return on shares, as well as, the variance, which indicates the risk based on normal distribution. The concept of normal distribution is based on two numbers. One is the average or expected return; the other is the variance or standard deviation.[137] The premise to this theory is that that returns are normally distributed. It must be stated here that variance reflects the potential risks that a certain portfolio inhabits. Both measures are depicted below.

---

[132] Cf. Gibson (2000), p. 8
[133] Cf. Myers (2003), pp.187
[134] Cf. Steiner (2007), p. 15
[135] Cf. Wellner (2003), p. 54
[136] Cf. Economist (2009 bb), p. 71
[137] Cf. Myers (2003), p.187

Portfolio Return	Portfolio Risk
$$\mu_p = \sum_{i=1}^{n} x_i \mu_i$$	$$\sigma_p^2 = \frac{1}{T} \sum_{t=1}^{T} (R_{pt} - \mu_p)^2$$

μ_p	Portfolio return	σ_p^2	Variance of the return
x_i	Part of security i on the total portfolio return	T	Number of observed returns
μ_i	Expected value of return, based on security i	R_{pt}	Portfolio return in period t
n	Number of securities of the portfolio	μ_p	Expected value of return, based on security i

(Own creation)

Figure 17: Markowitz's Portfolio return and Portfolio risk

The optimal portfolio is a combination of return (μ) and risk (σ) with three premises:[138]

- No other portfolio has a lower risk with the same return

- No other portfolio has a higher return at the same risk

- No other portfolio has a higher expected value of return and a lower risk
Furthermore, Markowitz assumes that there are no transaction costs and taxes, every security is divisible, and the timeframe is always a full period. The optimal portfolio can be found on an efficiency curve, which is depicted below.

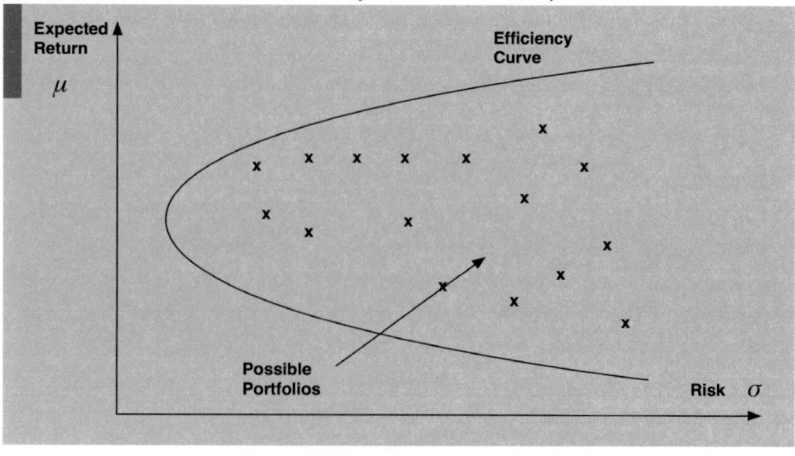

(Own creation)

Figure 18: Efficiency Curve[139]

---

[138] Cf. Steiner (2007), p. 8
[139] Cf. Steiner (2007), p. 9

The x-marked spots represent all possible risk-return combinations, but only the combinations on the efficiency curve are relevant for the investor. To estimate the efficiency curve, the covariance of the single variances is needed, as illustrated below.

$$COV_{ij} = \frac{1}{T} \sum_{t=1}^{T} (R_{it} - \mu_i)(R_{jt} - \mu_j)$$

COV_{ij}	Covariance of the security return i and j
R_{it}	Return of security i in period t
$\mu_{i,j}$	Expected return of security i,j
T	Number of periods

(Own creation)

Figure 19:Covariance of the portfolio[140]

The popularity of this theory is immense, because it diversifies or eliminates systematic risks out of a portfolio. Even though, there is still a rest of risk. In this regard, the risk of a Black Swan, which is an unexpected event in the market, introduced in chapter 1, cannot be eliminated.

This is not the only criticism to the theory. Especially the application of this model is not very practical.[141] Only if the historical development of a security is well known, then future estimations are possible. Concerning the discussion of GETs, experts criticize this model, because it does not incorporate trading costs, makes too many simplified assumptions, and investors are not that rational as the model assumes. This is the field of behavioral finance.[142] However, this problem can be solved, by applying an indices model to the theory, which is also called the Sharpe Index model.[143] The model provides indices, which help to estimate the efficiency curve of the portfolio according to a share index. Finally, even though that there is criticism to the Markowitz model, this is the most popular model, and is the foundation for further developments, like CAPM[144]. Until new models are proven, this model is still the valid model for diversifying risks in a portfolio.

---

[140] Cf. Steiner (2007), p. 14
[141] The Economist (2009 h)
[142] Cf. Pompian (2006), p. 6
[143] Cf. Steiner (2007), p. 15
[144] Cf. Steiner (2007), p.15

3.4.3.2 Capital Asset Price Model (CAPM)

CAPM has been developed by Sharpe, Lintner and Mossin, and is based in the portfolio selection theory of Markowitz.[145] It also incorporates the approach of diversifying risk, which is known as residual risk, or alpha.[146] However, it goes further by asking which part of the risk cannot be diversified. In this case, the hypothesis is that it is even risky to hold a basket of all shares in the market.[147] An investor has always the change to go for safety treasury bills, but he has to be rewarded for taking a risk. The question is therefore, how much a particular asset depends on the market development, when alpha risk has been eliminated. Market volatility is incorporated by beta, which connects the market risk, and the potential revenue.[148] Based on the capital market line, the standard equation for CAPM can be derived, as depicted below.

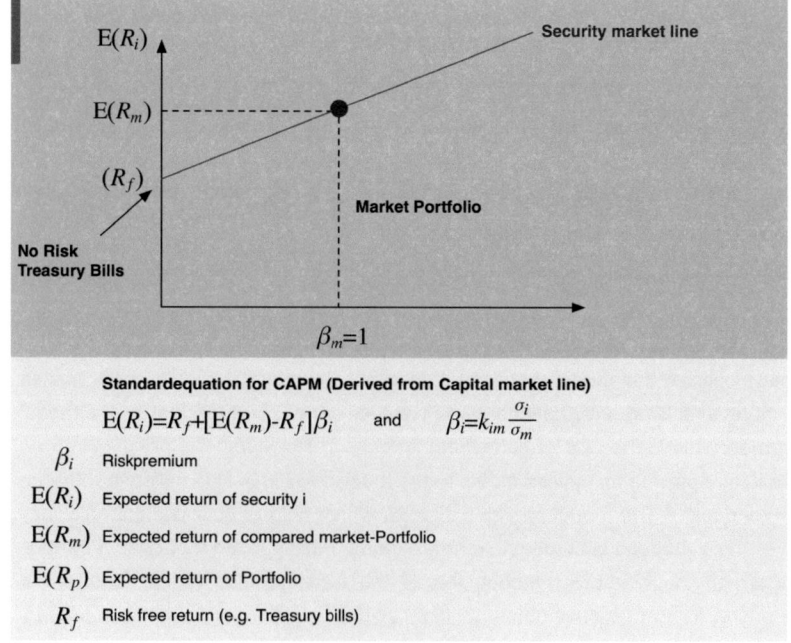

Standardequation for CAPM (Derived from Capital market line)

$$E(R_i)=R_f+[E(R_m)-R_f]\beta_i \quad \text{and} \quad \beta_i=k_{im}\frac{\sigma_i}{\sigma_m}$$

β_i Riskpremium

$E(R_i)$ Expected return of security i

$E(R_m)$ Expected return of compared market-Portfolio

$E(R_p)$ Expected return of Portfolio

R_f Risk free return (e.g. Treasury bills)

(Own creation)

Figure 20:CAPM[149]

---

[145] Cf. Steiner (2007), p. 21
[146] Cf. Bishop (2009), p.48
[147] Cf. Bishop (2009, p.49
[148] Cf. Rolfes (2003), p.38
[149] Cf. Steiner (2007), p. 26

As CAPM indicates, with a higher systematic (alpha) risk the possibility of gained returns of a security are also higher, which is a fundamental statement for value based management and portfolio management.[150] Therefore, the return of an investments project is deeply connected to the risk that has to be taken.[151] Central Costs of investment related to the specific risk are capital costs. This leads to the fundamental statement, that every (investment)-project has its own capital costs, and there can be no adjusted capital costs in the corporation. This relation is depicted below, concerning the weighted average cost of capital

$$k_{EC} = r_f + \beta \cdot (r_M - r_f) \qquad WACC = k_{EC}\frac{EC}{OC} + k_{DC}\frac{DC}{OC}$$

r_f Risk-free Rate $\qquad k_{EC}$ Weighted Equity Expense Ratio

r_M Market Return $\qquad k_{DC}$ Weighted Debt Expense Ratio

β Volatitlity

(Own creation)

Figure 21: Weighted equity expense ration and WACC

Again, there is criticism to the theory.[152] First, the availability of a zero-risk option (treasury bonds) is eyed critically.[153] Second, experts say that the market portfolio cannot be calculated or estimated sufficiently. However, this model has the ability to show the interdependence between risk and return.[154] To conclude the analysis of portfolio theory, the third approach the arbitrage pricing theory (APT) must be mentioned shortly, which has been invented by Ross. Theoretically, this approach may ha a benefit compared to CAPM. Even though it must be stated here, that CAPM is by far the more used model. A reason is that APT does not incorporate economical influence to the risk factor.

Finally, the market portfolio theory is a solid basis for risk diversification. Even though, there is criticism to the theory. An interesting point of Taleb is: "If you remove their Gaussian assumptions and treat prices as scalable, you are left with hot air."[155] Spreemann reasons that if the people do not act according to the portfolio theory they must be cleverer.[156] The hypothesis of this paper is that only a combination of profound risk analysis in combination with mathematical methods is profound enough to reduce a possible risk to an absolute minimum.

---

[150] Cf. Spreemann (2006), p.317
[151] Cf. Spreemann (2006), p. 318
[152] Cf. Steiner (2007), p. 34
[153] Cf. Steiner (2007), p.28
[154] Cf. Brealey (2003), p. 189
[155] Cf. Taleb (2007), p. 277
[156] Cf. Spreemann (2006), p. 355

3.4.4 Business Portfolio management

The core elements of strategic business portfolio planning tools are the Boston Consulting Matrix (BCG) or the McKinsey Matrix that determine growth and share of the current business portfolio, and give reasons for decision-making.

By means of qualitative analysis, tools and measures of business portfolio management focus on strategic management decisions that determine the value proposition of business. Based on the analysis of global economic trends, it can be asserted that economic growth will develop more slowly, or even stagnate, in developed economies in the next decades.[157] Therefore, Business portfolio management must consider this development. Based on this assumption, this chapter reflects how selected business portfolio frameworks can be complemented into business planning.

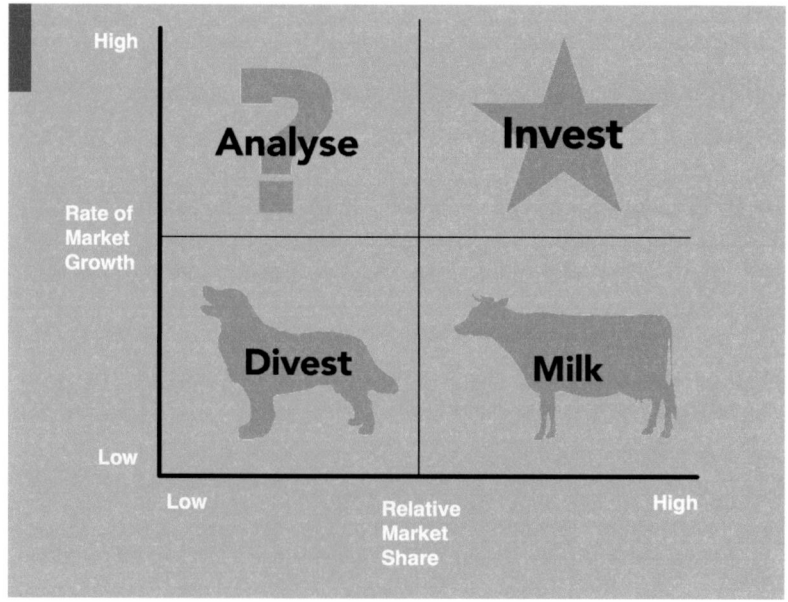

(Own creation)

Figure 22: BCG Matrix[158]

The above figure depicts the BCG-Matrix, which can be applied to SBUs, products, or business segments, within a company. It determines the relative market share and rate of market growth of an individual group of assets. The

---

[157] Cf. Economist (2009 e), p. 71
[158] Cf. Stern (2006), p.260

outcome of the analysis is a variety of strategic options. The range goes from whether an asset is worth for further investments, or if it should be divested. The key to a successful portfolio is a set of diversified assets with different growth rates and different market shares.[159] It must be stated here that in times of crisis, the view on the corporate portfolio can be blurred, because growth rates decline. Latter is caused by a breakdown of markets or economies. In this case, the management needs to observe current market activities, especially the movements of opponents, to determine the real position of the portfolio asset. The further development of the BCG Matrix is the GE Matrix, as depicted below.

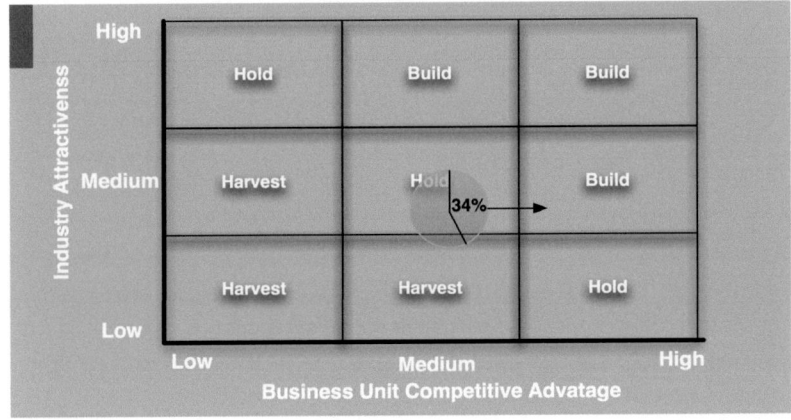

(own creation)
Figure 23: GE Matrix[160]

The axis industry attractiveness is computed on market size, market growth, and inflation recovery, which ability to cover cost increases by higher productivity and increased prices, and the business unit competitive advantage axis is computed on market position, competitive position, and return on sales.[161] Each circle represents a SBU. The size of circle represents the market size, the size of the pie reflects the market share, and the arrow is indicating the direction of the SBU development. In summary, this toolset helps to refine the business analysis based on the current position of business.

---

[159] Cf. Stern (2006), p.261
[160] Cf. Grant (2005), p.493
[161] Cf. Grant (2005), p.493

3.5   GET Assessment Framework

The crucial point to Corporate Development is how to encounter the impact of global economic trends, and how to establish preemptive measures that absorb the negative power on economic growth. Based on literature research, the following framework gives guidance for managers on how to detect bottlenecks, and how to establish short-term and long-term measures. This assessment framework, as depicted below, is the bridge between the analysis of corporate development and change management. The steps that are depicted within the illustration are explained throughout this chapter.

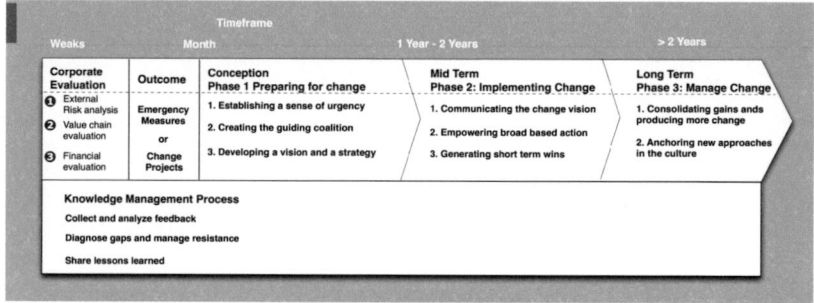

(Own creation, based on AT Kirney)

Figure 24: Assessment of GETs[162]

Beginning with the corporate evaluation, the current power of a GET in regard to business development is estimated. This evaluation should be included in the strategic planning process of the corporation. By incorporating the risk configuration, the strategic positioning, as well as, financial aspects concerning liquidity and credibility, possible measures to protect the competitive position of the portfolio can be determined. Risk analysis (1) refers to qualitative risk analysis, which is illustrated in the next sub-chapter. Its core is to estimate how possible risk can be identified and incorporated into the strategic planning process. The point strategic position (2) is focused on analyzing the actual business portfolio, concerning the value chain. (3) Refers to financial analysis that determines the degree of liquidity. The outcome of this short-term analysis, are possible emergency measures that need to be implemented instantly, as well as, a long-term change projects that restructure the corporate portfolio.

---

[162] Cf. Rothenbücher (2009), p 5

3.5.1   Risk analysis

Unanticipated and incalculable events raise the degree of uncertainty for business planning, because they directly influence the risk factor of the corporate portfolio. The portfolio risk is a key driver for company strategists and therefore the economic changes are a key challenge for global corporate development of an organization.[163] First, the analysis stresses the worst-case scenario of risk, the bankruptcy of companies. This should encourage the reader to understand the urgency for sufficient risk management. As business experts at AT Kirney (2009) found out there are several reasons for the bankruptcy of corporations, as depicted below.[164]

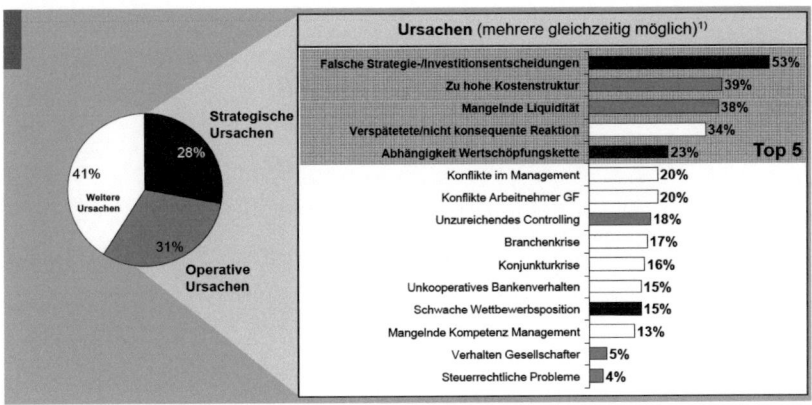

(Own creation, based on AT Kirney (2009))

Figure 25: Reasons for bankruptcy[165]

Under the top 5 reasons, which are bankruptcy due to wrong (a) strategy and investment decision, (b) wrong cost structure, (c) lack of liquidity, (d) dependencies in-between value chains, or (e) the late or not consequent decision-making.[166] Latter reason leads to the hypothesis that companies do acknowledge changes, but are not competent enough to handle these. In case of GETs, management needs to be prepared beforehand for deep changes in the economy of tomorrow to stay competitive. The new economic environment needs to be perceived early, so there can be enough time for change measures. This also confirms the importance for the next chapter Change Management.

---

[163] Cf. Kottler (2002), p. 32
[164] Cf. Rothenbücher (2009), p. 3
[165] Cf. AT Kearney (2009), p. 6
[166] Cf. Rothenbücher(2009), p.2

3.5.1.1 Risk cycle

Every corporation is enclosed to a complex environment that has risks to the business.[167] In order to incorporate risks into qualitative portfolio management, the following approach should be applied.

(Own creation)[168]

Figure 26: Risk cycle

As depicted above, the risk cycle begins with risk identification (1). As an example concerning GETs, chapter 1 of this paper identified the top seven trends, which are indeed a risk to corporations. Next, these trends need to be quantified (2). This involves detailed information to judge how deep the effect is, which can be depicted as a risk vs. return curve. The more information is available; the lower is the degree of uncertainty. If the information has been collected, then the risk to corporations is evaluated (3). Strategic assessment, as well as, value chain analysis depicts which levels of the organization, and which parts of the business are mostly affected. These tools are given within this chapter. Finally, monitoring of the risk shows how the development is influencing the business (4). This requires that the corporate culture perceives the risks and is aware if changes are happening.

---

[167] Cf. Bea (2001), p. 108
[168] Cf. Bea (2001), p.109

3.5.1.2 Value chain evaluation

The activities that are required to produce a product or to conduct a service can be aligned as a value chain. Every corporation has, according to Porter, an individual value added chain that is embedded in a larger stream of activities.[169] The combination of these individual value chains from upstream to downstream is perceived as a value system, which is depicted below.

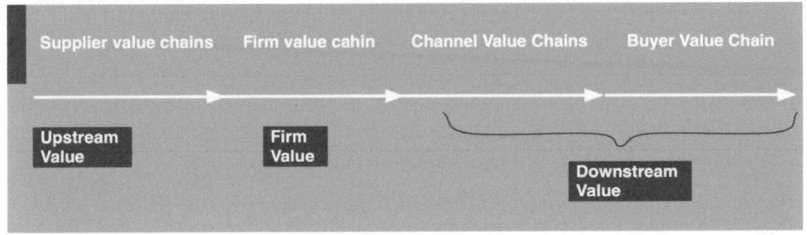

(own creation, based on Porter)

Figure 27: Porter's Value System[170]

Therefore, competitive advantage of a corporation is not only depended on its individual value chain performance, but also on the performance of its stakeholder's value chain performance. This was particular evident in the automobile industry during the credit crunch. As the sales of big automobile retailers went down, the supplier industry suffered, and many companies went out of business. That has a negative effect on the manufacturers and retailers, who needed to find new partners for their business.[171] This strategic connection from company to its stakeholders is called system-environment-fit.[172] Each SBU of a MNC has its own value system according to their product or service. In this regard, the company, suppliers, and channels all benefit through better recognition and exploitation of such linkages.[173] Concerning GETs, these linkages provide potentials, as well as, risks. The automobile industry is a good example for the risk that arises out of a financial crisis for all players among the value system. From the perspective of a manufacturing company, the risk can be diversified, if the MNC establishes relationships with different suppliers and exploits new channels to downstream their product to the buyer. The most important evaluation of possible threats is the analysis of the internal value chain, which can be perceived as a system of activities inside the company involved in the value creation.

---

[169] Cf. Porter (1998), p.78
[170] Cf. Porter (1998), p.78
[171] Cf. Turner (2008)
[172] Cf. Bea (2001), p.114
[173] Cf. Porter (1998), p.79

Primary and secondary activities can be grouped into two categories called administration and achievement, as depicted below.

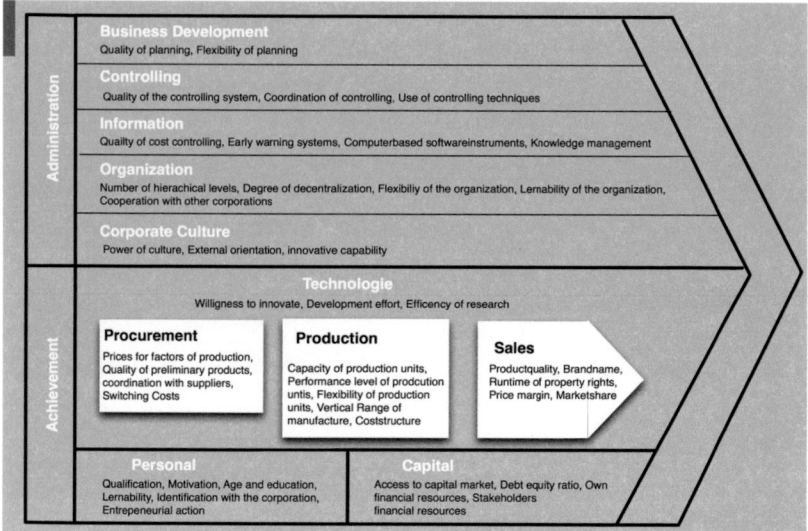

(Own creation, based on Bea and Porter)

Figure 28:Strategic value chain[174]

Administration is aimed at the activities within the company that incorporate "softfactors" of the business, like corporate development, controlling, information, organization, and corporate culture. Achievement points at the "hard-factors" of the company that are directly involved in the production or service process. These factors are the operational activities technology, procurement, production, or service, sales, personal and capital.[175]

In the figure attributes to each of these activities are given. In the wider sense, the short-term analysis of the GET assessment framework should assess possible bottlenecks concerning activities. In the narrower sense, each of the strategic potentials (attributes) of the value chain should to be analyzed. Each SBU in the company holds its own value chain. Therefore, each of these value chains has to be analyzed. Regarding the business development planning process, this qualification, and quantification has to be done by the management of the SBUs.

---

[174] Cf. Bea (2001), p. 132
[175] Cf. Porter (1998), p.314

3.5.1.3 Financial Evaluation

The core problem of business operations is to assure that enough liquidity is provided to finance the investments in the short-term and in the long-term. Especially during big investments, like a merger or acquisition, companies need to have enough capital to process the transaction in time, but they also need enough capital to finance their short-term investments. The short-term availability of liquidity can be estimated with two liquidity ratios, which are depicted below.

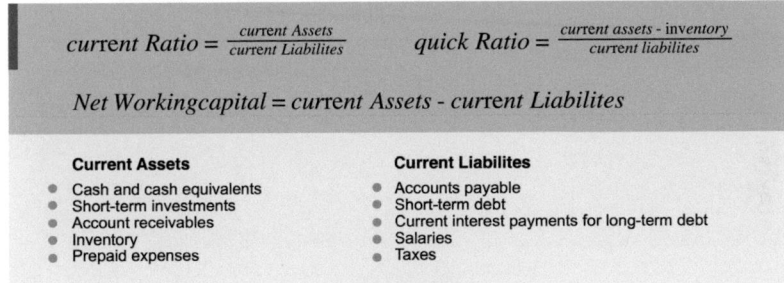

$$current\ Ratio = \frac{current\ Assets}{current\ Liabilites} \qquad quick\ Ratio = \frac{current\ assets - inventory}{current\ liabilities}$$

$$Net\ Workingcapital = current\ Assets - current\ Liabilites$$

Current Assets
- Cash and cash equivalents
- Short-term investments
- Account receivables
- Inventory
- Prepaid expenses

Current Liabilites
- Accounts payable
- Short-term debt
- Current interest payments for long-term debt
- Salaries
- Taxes

(Own creation)

Figure 29: Liquidity Ratio

The current ratio is simply the relationship between current assets and current liabilities, which are short-term debt that need to be paid within 12 month, as well as, long-term debt.[176] Supposedly, the higher the ratio the more liquidity is available in the company. However, this is only a crude measure, because it does not account the liquidity of current assets.[177] As a rule of thumb this ratio must be 1:1, 2:1 for current ratio, but to have a sufficient meaning these ratios need to be compared to other companies in the same industry, or can be used to illustrate the development of a company.[178] The quick ratio excludes inventory, because it is not convertible into cash quickly.[179]

It must be stated here that the analysis of the working capital is the most important. To analyze the role of inventory, the working capital needs to be analyzed. As depicted above, the net working capital can be calculated based on current assets and current liabilities. A positive value indicates that current liabilities are financed in the long run, where as a negative value indicates that long-term investments are financed with short-term debt.[180]

---

[176] Cf. Friedlob, G. T. (2008), p. 159
[177] Cf. Van Horne (2005), p.139
[178] Cf. Friedlob, G. T. (2008), p.160
[179] Cf. Friedlob, G. T. (2008), p.159
[180] Cf. Meyer (2007), p. 26

3.5.1.4 Results of the short term analysis

If the analysis of the assessment framework, as depicted above, results in potential dangers to the corporate portfolio, then the company has several options to react. First, each of the risks that arise out of the value chain analysis, and the financial analysis should be depicted in a simple management framework, to clearly distinct between urgency and importance of a risk, as depicted below.

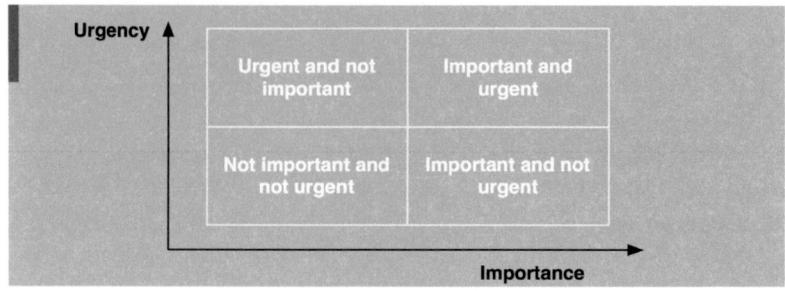

(Own creation)

Figure 30: Urgency and Importance framework[181]

Risks that are estimated as urgent and important need to be approached emergently, whereas risks that are important and not urgent can be encountered by establishing counter measures that are implemented with a long-term change management project. In conclusion, this framework helps the analyst to find the optimal strategic levers that needs to be applied to the portfolio of the corporation. These levers are solutions that can be implemented at a specific part of a SBU value chain, or to the overall company portfolio.

The assessment framework distinguishes between emergency measures, which should be implemented directly, and the long-term change measures, that reshape the configuration of the corporation. In this case, the degree of urgency determines the measure that should be implemented. Measures can vary from (1) turnaround measures for crises-driven companies,[182] (2) working capital management, (3) technological changes, and (4) long-term structural changes.

In conclusion, the urgency and importance framework is a measure to refine the estimated risks concerning their significance to the actual business position. It should help Corporate Development officers, to estimate the real relevance of a GET, and to time levers of strategic measures.

---

[181] Cf. El-Erian (2008), p.290
[182] Cf. Thompson (2008), p. 257

3.5.2 Change Management

This subchapter introduces the methodologies of change management (CM), which are used to implement countermeasures in the long-term. A relatively new discipline has evolved from a set of practical, descriptive, and prescriptive theories to a discipline with models and toolsets.[183] Status quo of literature is that change management is a wide field of research with individual models, which describe the topic, regarding to the preference and knowledge of the author, as well as, the time they have been evaluated. Even though, each of the approaches consist with the fact that individual change is at the heart of everything that is achieved in organizations.[184] With the individual motivation to change, the environment is able to change, not the other way around. To successfully implement a change process, profound methodologies of CM are needed.

In order to handle the impact of GETs, corporations need to be prepared for long-term structural changes, and need to implement them even before they occur. Hence, CM is a crucial challenge for all organizations.[185] A study by Capgemini and Ernst&Young reveils that a usable change management toolset has a flexible character, because change projects are usually conducted one-time and their repeatability is not given.[186] Therefore, it is even more important that knowledge that was gained through a change process is incorporated into the corporate culture.

The impact of GETs on the development of markets and industries drives the need for major changes within organizations. Even though, if change is perceived as urgent depends on the business strategy of the responsible management. It is the prisoner's dilemma between short-term economic growth and sustainable development. Therefore, it is priority to the top management and the corporate development unit of a company to decide the route of change, because this may involve a loss in shareholder value. Especially the GET of Climate Change makes it is obvious that emerging countries neglect change in this case, and tend to prefer economic growth at any cost.[187] Even though, sustainability is top priority to western corporations, because they raise the value of Corporate Identity, and they lead to a reduction of operating costs, because processes are optimized and less energy is consumed.[188]

---

[183] Cf. Nilikant (2007), p.18
[184] Cf. Cameron (2004), p. 9
[185] Cf. Cohen (2002), p. 1
[186] Cf. Baumöl (2008), p.3
[187] Cf. The Economist (2009 i)
[188] Cf. Lohnes (2008)

Even more, the people within the corporation must have the will to conduct the change. According to Michael Jarrett, the discipline of Change Management addresses the process of change within the organization, but the belief or the assumption that change is manageable top-down leads to faulty interventions.[189] Therefore, CM has two components the organizational change itself, and the change of people within the environment. Latter is the crucial element to success.

Thus, a successful application of change management needs to integrate the people within the organization, and even more, changes to the organization need to be inline with the values of the corporation. Without this strategic fit, changes will not be effective and can cause serious harm to the corporation. For example, frame-breaking change involves (a) a new definition or modification of the companies' core values, (b) an alteration of the distribution of power, (c) a modification in structure, systems and procedures, or (d) change in the way that people work together within the organization.[190]

Methods that are used within industries are numerous; they range from very structured business reengineering approaches until unstructured methodologies that focus on the social and emotional component of change.[191] In the narrower sense, change management covers several measures that can be applied, which are[192]:

- Business Process Reengineering
- Restructuring
- Quality Programs
- Mergers and Acquisitions
- Strategic Changes
- Cultural Changes
- Political Work

Each of the above measure affects the value configuration within the company. Therefore, change management may be defined as a process-orientated approach to lock in the strategic targets for executives who conduct a change process within the organization.

---

[189] Cf. Crainer (2004), p. 834
[190] Cf. Nilakant (2007), p.47
[191] Cf. Baumöl (2008), p.1
[192] Cf. Kottler (2002), p.19

CM should be part of the strategic planning process, and needs to be incorporated into the business planning of CD to gain the most acceptances in the corporation and to generate the highest benefit. Successful change management projects are based on a carefully outlined plan of the whole change process, before the change is conducted. The most famous and most cited approach of change management approach is the approach of John P. Kotter.

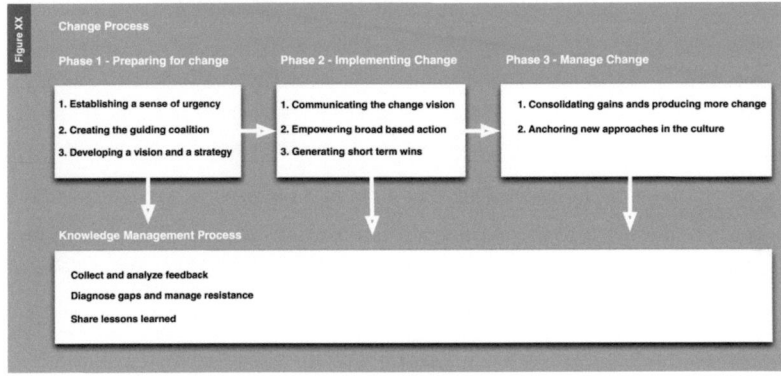

(Own creation)

Figure 31: Change Management Process

Above figure shows an excerpt of the get assessment framework, to expose the steps for further analysis. The whole approach is divided into a change process and a knowledge management process. Arrows within the picture represent the flow of information between the process phases and the knowledge management process. The CM process is based on the approach by Kotter, which is enhanced by grouping the steps of the eight-step process into phases that represent the state of the change process, according to their progress and their completion time.

It contains the planning, the short-term implementing, and the long-term establishment of structural change measures. In relation to the work of Coscy, there are a few key principles when applying a process model of change. Every step is necessary (a) states that each of the steps is needed to provide a solid basis for the change.[193] The process is dynamic (b), which means that large-scale transformation is never straightforward.[194] Furthermore, change is an iterative process, and steps within the process can happen simultaneously (c).[195]

---

[193] Cf. Cohen (2002), p.5
[194] Cf. Cohen (2002), p.6
[195] Cf. Cohen (2002), p.7

A Knowledge Management (KM) process that accompanies the change complements the whole process. Two benefits can be gained by this methodology. First, knowledge, which is gained within the Change Process, can be refined and inherited by the knowledge workers within the company. Therefore, information is exchanged throughout the whole corporation and in-between the management levels. A side effect, by incorporating the people within the company, the acceptance for the change process should be as high as possible, and there is an effect on the corporate culture. Second, decision-making can be enhanced because people can interact online without a time constraint. Information can be accessed and communicated faster. Moreover, researchers postulate that it should be insured that the process of change is well documented, monitored, and communicated throughout the organization.[196] This can be achieved by this methodology.

3.5.2.1 Preparing for change

3.5.2.1.1 Establishing a sense of urgency

A sense of urgency is crucial to gaining needed corporation for a change process.[197] Especially in MNCs people tend to stay in their comfort-zone, and need to be triggered externally in order to be conduct a change.

In this sense, urgency reflects the need to change, which depends on situation in which the corporation is. For example, if the business is running of base, then the need for change is occasionally higher then if the business runs well. Therefore, there are some premises to the success of a change project:

- Create the environment to change
- Every affected member of the corporation should be directly involved in the change process.
- Change Management projects need to be inline with the corporate strategy
- Commitment between the strategic levels of an MNC is needed, and cannot be a simple presentation of the top-level management.[198]
- Leaders have to reduce fear, anger, and complacency in their corporation to gain the widest acceptance.[199]
- Establish a new process in the knowledge management system

---

[196] Cf. Kotter (2002), p. 48
[197] Cf. Kotter (1999), p. 36
[198] Cf. Groten (2007), p. 364
[199] Cf. Cohen (2002), p.3

3.5.2.1.2 Creating the guiding coalition

Because structural changes are hard to acquire, a broad coalition is needed to sustain the process. According to Kotter, there are three premises in creating a coalition that makes changes happen.[200] Finding the right people (a) is the first premise in the coalition building. This involves finding people with leadership skills that have strong position power, broad experience, and high credibility. To achieve best results, trust has to be created (b). Team building activities like side-events or joint activities in general help to raise the team spirit, and create a healthy culture. Finally, the management team needs to develop a common goal (c). Latter has to be so strong that it should be sensible to the head and appealing to the heart.[201] To strengthen the perception of goals, change targets, vision, and strategy should be defined in the knowledge management system.

3.5.2.1.3 Developing a vision and a strategy

Urgency is the trigger for change, but vision and strategy are needed to steer the action into the right direction,[202] as well as, to break the resistance within the corporate environment.[203] A good vision is capable to be the leitmotif or the central theme for actions that are conducted during the change process.[204] Developing a vision is never achieved in a single meeting, it is difficult, and sometimes an emotionally charged experience.[205] To develop a feasible strategic vision for a change process, the following model by Kotter should be used.[206]

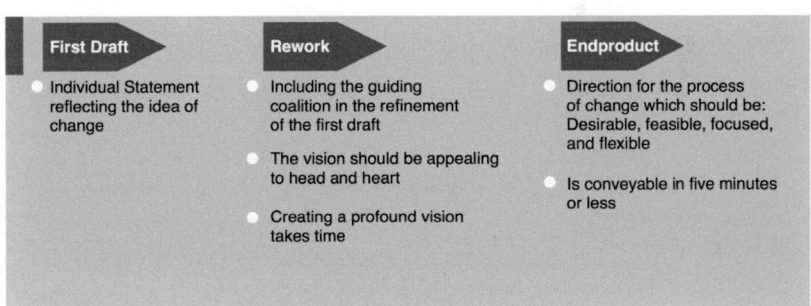

(Own creation, based on Kotter)

Figure 32: Develop a Vision and Strategy

---

[200] Cf. Kotter (1999), p. 66
[201] Cf. Kotter (1999), p. 66
[202] Cf. Cohen (2002), p. 63
[203] Cf. Kotter (2002), p. 69
[204] Cf. Stolzenberg (2009), p. 14
[205] Cf. Esther Cameron, p. 147
[206] Cf. Kotter (2002), p. 81

3.5.2.2 Implementing change

3.5.2.2.1 Communicating the change vision

As Kotter stated, "The real power of a vision is unleashed only when … [the] enterprise … [has] a common understanding of its goals and direction."[207] Hence, a vision is most effective if a broad base of employees understand its purpose, and the direction of change. Even more, if the intense and the direction of change are not understood, change will not happen.[208] Therefore, the corporation needs to avoid under communicating the vision. Especially with the use of IT systems, managers tend to perceive that data transfer is enough to successfully communicate a vision, but good communication is far away from data transfer.[209] A vision statement is information with an emotional touch. It may address anxiety because it is intended to overcome resistance.

Moreover, it is an exchange of knowledge that involves learning. Information can be consumed without a deeper understanding, vis-à-vis, knowledge needs adequate communication, otherwise it is not understood, and no action will take place. Change can only happen, if employees understand the intense and meaning of change, and are willing to change the way of their actual thinking.

3.5.2.2.2 Empowering broad-based action

To empower broad-based action requires leadership skills by the change manager, because it requires the logical understanding of how the vision can be achieved, as depicted below.

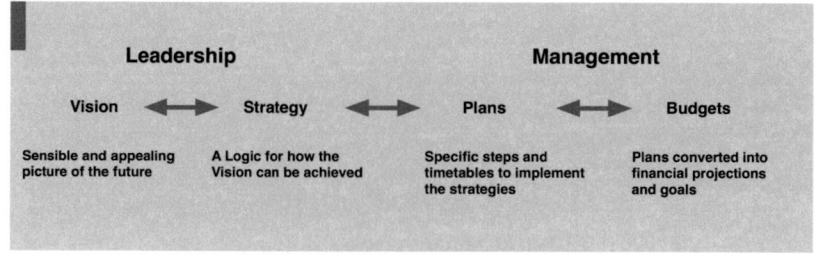

(Own creation, based on Kotter)[210]

Figure 33:Leadership vs. Management

---

[207] Cf. Kotter (2002), p. 85
[208] Cf. Kostka (2009), p. 19
[209] Cf. Cohen (2007), p. 84
[210] Cf. Kotter (1996), p.71

Kotter and Cohen give four crucial points to the success of empowering broad based-action.[211] Another element of creating the guiding coalition is finding individuals with change experience who are able to motivate people (a). These people should have a strong leadership skill and may be found within the corporation. In addition, creating a recognition and reward system (b) promotes positive reaction to change and empowers the will to continue with the change process. This is important, because structural change is long lasting.

Feedback (c) is probably the most important aspect. It gives people, who are involved in the progress, guidance how they can adopt to meet the requirements of the new situation. The mechanism of feedback can also be linked with the knowledge management process, which is illustrated later in the analysis. If the blockades by established managers are too strong, (d) they have to be replaced, otherwise the change effort is worthless

3.5.2.2.3 Generating short-term wins

Structural changes invoke a psychological reaction by the employees. This reaction can be structured into a seven-phase model, which is depicted below.

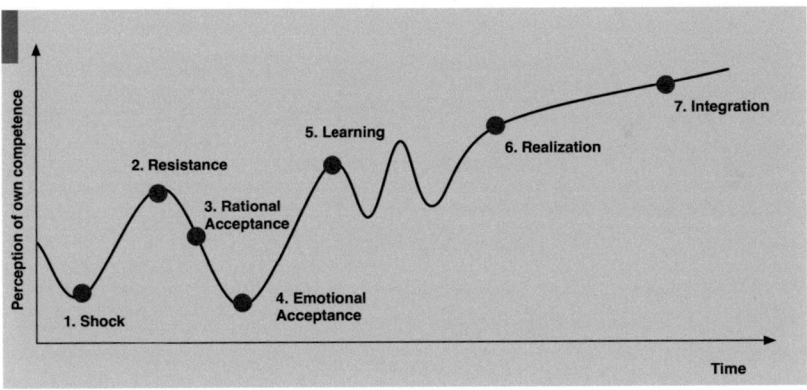

(Own creation, based on Claudia Kostka, Annette Mönch)

Figure 34: Psychological effect of a change process[212]

The expansion of the curve is related to the deepness of business transformation. If a structural change is happening, then the occurrence-time of each point within the illustration shifts to the left or right side of the diagram. The crucial point in acceptance of the implementation of changes lies in points 1-4 of the learning process. Every change causes a shock (1) inside the employees; because change

---

[211] Cf. Cohen (2007), p. 123
[212] Cf. Kostka (2009), p. 13

drives people out of their comfort zones, and the natural reaction (2) is resistance. Short term-wins help employees to rationally (3), to emotionally (4) accept, and to empower the effectiveness of transformation. Depending on the deepness of change, short-term goals should be planned and achieved within one or two years, otherwise, the transformation will not be accepted, and the transformation will decline.[213] Only if short-term goals are successful, people within the organization are willing to learn (5) and inherit the new circumstances (6 – 7). Short-term goals help the people to cope with the change, because they will see the benefit.

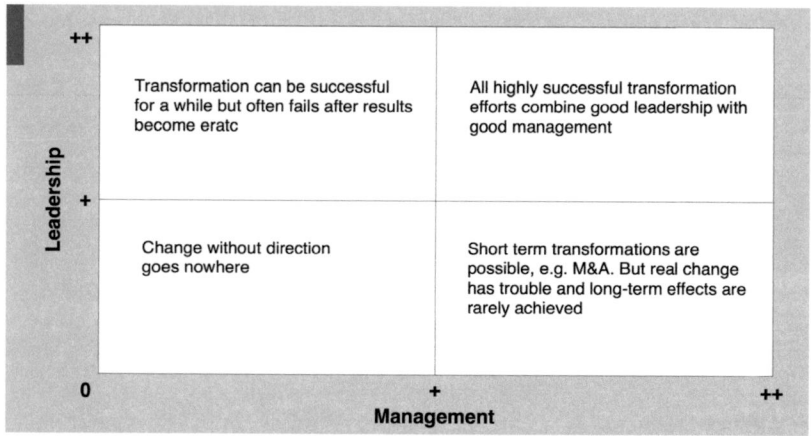

(Own creation, based on Kottter)

Figure 35: Relationship of Management and Leadership skills in regard to successful changes[214]

The above graphic finalizes the discussion about short-term goals and builds the bridge to the personal abilities required in long-term change projects. As depicted, a successful change project requires both good leadership and good management skills. First, both skills on their own may be successful for short-term goals, but for long-term transformation, leadership is necessary. Second, even though that leadership uteruses deeper transformation, management skills need to complement the more visionary skills for the establishment of long-term transformation, and to anchor the achievements within the corporate environment.

---

[213] Cf. Kotter (2002), p.120
[214] Cf. Kotter (2002), p.129

3.5.2.3 Managing Change

3.5.2.3.1 Consolidating gains and produce more change

Consolidating gains implicates that after a short-term win has been achieved, the change process should not stop, because more change can and has to be achieved. Many managers tend to declare victory too soon, which stops the momentum and can lead to a reversing progress.[215] Especially GETs, which have a long-term effect, effort the endurance of all employees to prepare for change in the long run. Especially CM programs that conclude many smaller change projects need to be orientated towards a long-term establishment of structural changes.[216] Four points according to Kotter can describe the success of such a major change effort.[217] (a) Credibility of short-term wins is used to tackle bigger projects, which indicates that a change management program should begin with the simple tasks, to gain short-term wins and to empower bigger change. If necessary, (b) Additional resources (people) are introduced into the change processes to help. Optional Change Managers from outside are able to support with leadership from below. This may be useful in case of too high resistance within the corporate environment. Senior management supports the change progress by keeping urgency up (c),[218] and by communicating the success throughout the company. In addition, interviews or publications in media help to demonstrate the awareness of certain issues to shareholders and stakeholders of the corporation. Finally, (d) unnecessary interdependencies should be reduced to ease the change.

3.5.2.3.2 Anchoring new approaches within the culture

If a change management project or program has been successful, changes should be implemented into the culture of the corporation. There are two ways how to integrate the newly gained knowledge into the corporation.[219] First, the corporate environment has to recognize how the new approaches, behaviors, and attitudes helped the business. This can be done through discussion, meetings, and presentations. It is worth mentioning that this approach is widely called "lessons learned" within the corporate dictionary. Second, the new concept has to be implemented into the further education measures of the company.

A new generation of leaders implements these measures into their daily life. This insures that these measures are practiced and refined during the work. Both

---

[215] Cf. Harvard Business School (2005), p. 81
[216] Cf. Smith (2004), p. 69
[217] Cf. Kotter (2002), p. 143
[218] Cf. Kotter (2002), p.143
[219] Cf. Kotter (1999), p. 90

approaches are also referred as "prove it" and "plan for succession".[220] Finally, the success of both measures depends on the quality of knowledge sharing within the company. The senior management of the company should insure that structural change transformations are rewarded and people are promoted. This measure tries to ensure that people start to orientate their work according to these examples.

3.5.3 Knowledge Management

3.5.3.1 Knowledge Capital within the Corporate Culture

In order to be successful, Organizations have to perceive that competitive success goes hand-in-hand with learning, but the dilemma is that "most people don't know how to learn" (Angyris 1991, p.81). According to Bukowitz, Knowledge Management (KM) is "the process by which the organization generates wealth from its intellectual or knowledge-based assets." (1999). Wealth or value is created in this context, when the company uses knowledge to achieve goals. The figure below depicts how knowledge management fits in the organizational context. If knowledge management and change management are connected, then knowledge capital is gained from every step within the change process, and changes are anchored in the corporate culture.

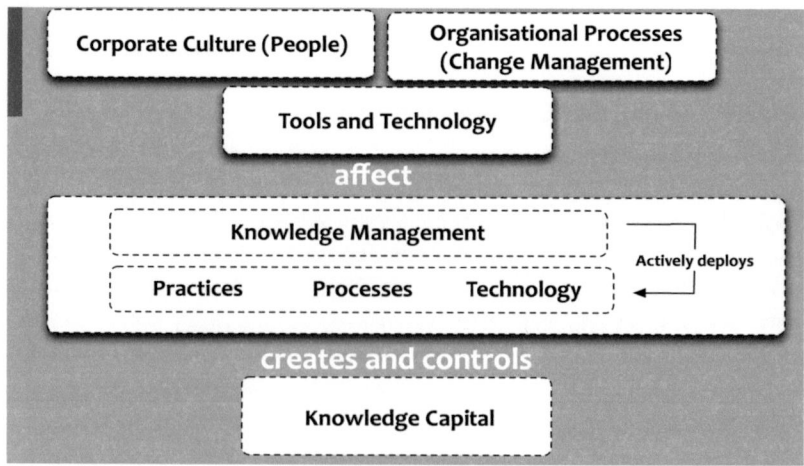

(Own creation, based on Awad 2005 p.3)

Figure 36: Knowledge Management[221]

---

[220] Cf. Harvard Business School (2005), p. 83
[221] Cf. Awad (2005), p.3

Organizational knowledge is the sum of knowledge-based assets, which may be defined as "anything valued without physical dimensions that is embedded in people or derived from processes, systems, and the culture associated within an organization [...]".[222] By definition, knowledge can be grouped into the personal or tacit knowledge and explicit knowledge. Latter is formal knowledge that can be transformed into information. Former is more important in the sense of change management. Tacit Knowledge is personal knowledge statements, domains of expertise, etc. it is embedded in individual experience and can be communicated in a direct and effective way.[223] This type of knowledge is most crucial in the sense of change management. Therefore, the main task has to be to transform tacit knowledge into explicit knowledge, and to incorporate it into a KM System.

3.5.3.2 Knowledge Management for Change Management

To successfully implement knowledge management for change management, there are some prerequisites to the scenario. First, the necessary IT infrastructure has to be provided, which should be not focused here. Second, and more crucial for change management, is to integrate people involved into a change process into this scenario. As the analysis of Kotter shows, successful change management projects have a strong focus on communication, and have a strong connection to the corporate culture.[224] As a hypothesis, if a corporation practices knowledge management, then the outcome of the change processes can be incorporated more easily into the corporate culture. This can be achieved by integrating the responsible people, which are involved in the change process, also into the knowledge management process. The knowledge management process that is used in this approach has the purpose to collect and analyze feedback, to diagnose gaps and manage resistance, as well as, to share lessons learned. By incorporating people across all strategic levels into the knowledge management process, newly acquired insights about possible risks can be assessed in a very fast manner across all levels of the corporation.

The strategic lever is that business decision-making can be accomplished even faster, and the corporation is better protected against threats. Especially the development of the financial and the energy market is highly volatile. A knowledge management system helps to react faster, and to establish possible emergency measures against an occurring, and potential dangerous event. The role concept of knowledge management distinguishes between champions (1), managers (2),

---

[222] Cf. Bukowitz (1999), p. 2
[223] Cf. Awad (2002), p.19
[224] Cf. Kotter (2002), pp. 46

and workers (3).[225] These roles need to be matched to levels of the strategic planning process. Knowledge workers can be found at the operational level of the corporation. They are directly involved within the change process and provide the best insights about how effectively the change is progressing. Knowledge managers are people on the organizational level of the SBU. Their job is to ensure that necessary knowledge is integrated into the system, and to control the quality of knowledge. Furthermore, they help to reflect the determined risks to the environment of the SBU. Knowledge Champions are found at the level of the corporation. Their job is to process the knowledge gained from the IT system, and to derive information for the progress of the change process. Therefore, they are responsible for risk monitoring, risk evaluation, risk planning, and communication. If all strategic levels integrate their evaluation of the change process, and especially of the GET risks into a knowledge management system, knowledge is gained for the corporation, which is beneficial for the overall development of the overall business, as well as, for the development of change projects in several ways. Awad defines knowledge as the "understanding gained through experience or study".[226] In this regard, experience is incorporated into the corporate culture.

By this means, the common problem that knowledge about change processes is not integrated into the corporation (see 3.5.2) can be solved. This also raises the efficiency of learning within the corporate environment, because knowledge about change processes is available within the corporate IT system. There are two main benefits from this consequence. First, mistakes can be avoided more easily, because information is available. Second, new people within the organization can be integrated more easily into the change process. Especially in long change processes, people within the organization change. Reasons may be retirement, or job change. Due to the availability of information, these people can be integrated better into the corporate culture.

As demonstrated, the risk cycle is the approach on how to monitor risks in a continuous process. It involves steady processing of information. By incorporating the monitoring process into the knowledge management system, the efficiency of risk assessment is raised, and therefore, the success of the change management process is more probable. Financial and energy markets, which tend to high volatilities, need to be monitored steady to capture risks. The outcome of each monitoring cycle should be incorporated into a knowledge management system.

---

[225] Cf. Awad (2005), pp.75
[226] Cf. Awad (2005), p. 33

4   Scarcity of oil and its impact to Multinational Corporations

Concerning the analysis of global economic trends (see chapter one), the GET "Scarcity of Resources" is used exemplary to show the impact to a multinational cooperation. The reader must be informed that the VC is not depicted as a real corporation; therefore, no financial assets exist within the company. Therefore, the measures are described on a holistic level that fit into other existing environments.

The resource used in this case scenario is oil. To receive a reasonable outcome, the Case Study "World Oil Outlook" by the OPEC is the data basis for the development of oil.[227] In the wider sense, the case study provides a forecast for oil supply and demand until 2030, which is also used in this reference case. Beginning time for the case study is January 1 2010.

In the narrower sense, the case study provides detailed information for the upstream and the downstream processes of the oil industry. The data is presented in a worst case, best case, and trend scenario. Latter is used within the case study. This data is accompanied by the findings of chapter one, which already introduced the problematic of scarcity. Altogether, a broad palette of information is given to depict a possible development of the scarcity scenario, and possible risks to corporations.

Based on above-mentioned information, the GET Assessment framework is applied to identify the strategic levers for counter measures, which can be perceived as a foundation for change management projects. Developed strategies are exemplary implemented within VC, by illustrating how change management practices to the virtual corporations. Even though, it must be stated here that the focus of the evaluation is to clearly identify strategic levers that will shape the chemical industry of tomorrow, which are most important to business planning.

4.1   Corporate Evaluation

Based on theories introduced in chapter two (Corporate Development) the impact to a virtual corporation (VC) is visualized, by using the concept of corporate evaluation, which were introduced within the GET assessment framework. By this means, external risks are mapped to the internal environment of the corporation, and change management strategies to actively take countermeasures for the protection of the competitive advantage are developed. Countermeasures are divided into emergency, short-term, and long-term strategies, according to the timeframe of the given data basis.

---

[227] Cf. OPEC (2009)

4.1.1 Risk evaluation

To feed the supply of energy demand in the near future is the biggest problem that arises out of the scarcity of resources. The discussion about scarcer energy involves all type of energy sources that are used in the industrial and the private area. Energy sources are divided into primary and secondary energy, as depicted below.[228]

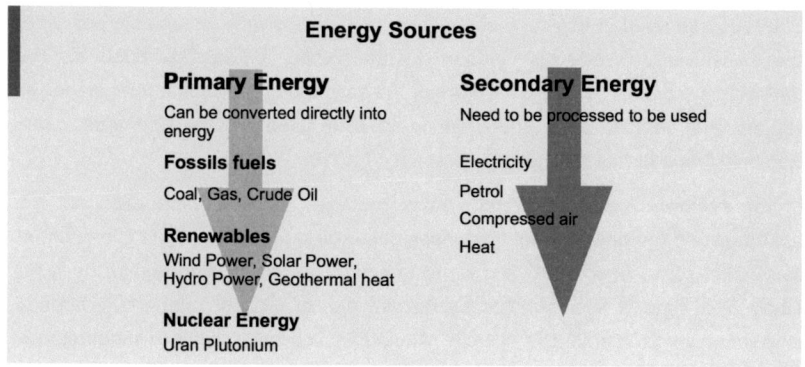

(Own Creation)

Figure 37: Energy Sources

Oil belongs to the group of primary energy. More precisely, it is part of the fossil fuels, which are coal, gas, and crude oil. Latter has played the central role during the age of industrialization and ensured the economic wealth and growth of economies. This problem has already been revealed within chapter one, and now the analysis has to be refined in order to illustrate what risks to existing industries arise out of this scenario.

To estimate possible risks, the oil demand, oil supply, and oil price development is processed, based on the data of the OPEC study, which illustrates exemplary how oil supply and demand may develop until 2030. In addition, the results gained from the general analysis of GETs are incorporated, as well. Where useful, additional data complements the analysis to raise the accuracy of the forecast. The external risks that arise out of this analysis are the foundation of the value chain evaluation and financial evaluation, which show the internal risks for the business operation.

---

[228] Cf. Doty (2009), p.4

4.1.1.1 Oil Demand

In the OPEC case study, data of the projection of the oil demand is sub-divided according to regions. In the figure below, this data is processed into an area diagram.

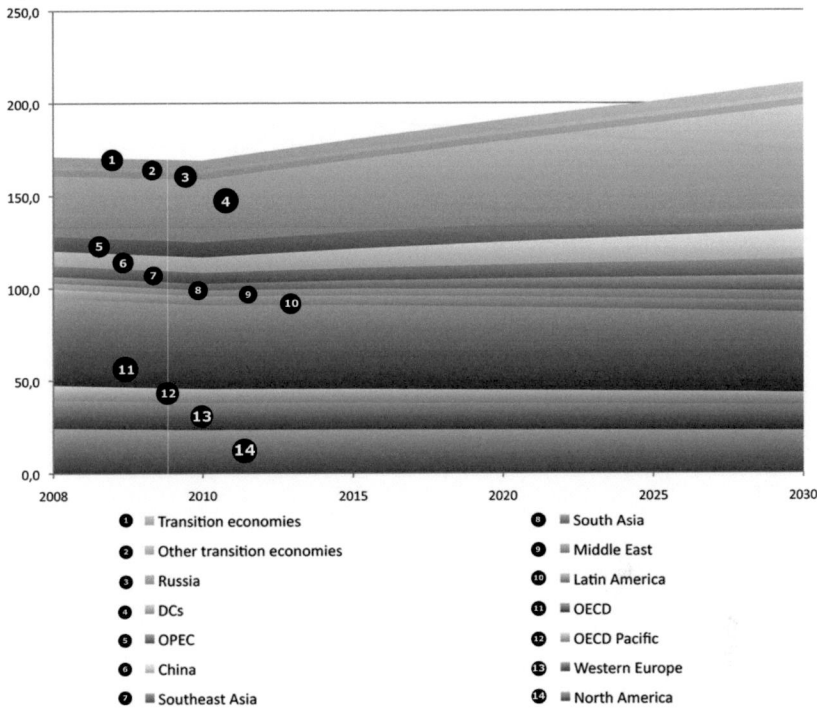

(Own creation based on OPEC data)

Figure 38: Oil demand development from 2008 until 2010 in mb/d [229]

This figure illustrates the rising demand of oil by the developing countries (DCs) and China, where as the demand of developed economies stays constant, and even falls slightly. 79% of the net growth in oil demand is in developing Asia.[230] Again, the forces of GETs are at work here. As illustrated in chapter one, the rising demand comes from the real GDP growth of these countries. The real GDP reflects the living standards, which will rise in the next decades. Consequently, there will be an increase in passenger cars, as well as, in commercial cars, as depicted below.

---

[229] Cf. OPEC (2009), p.53
[230] Cf. OPEC (2009), p.53

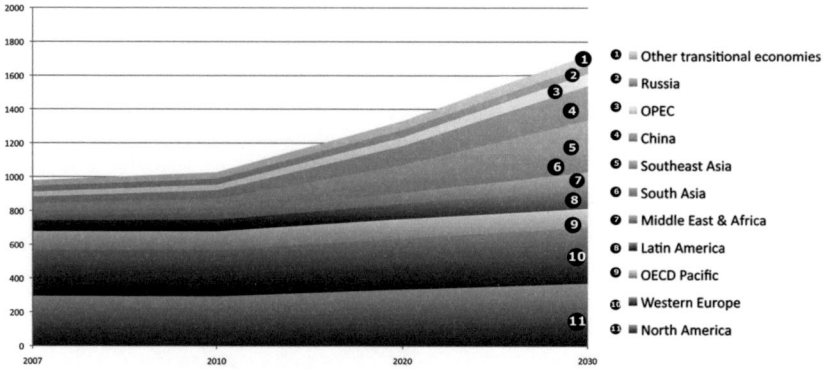

(Own creation, based on OPEC)

Figure 39: Volume of commercial and private cars from 2007 til 2030 (mio)[231]

All the growth in oil demand through 2030, and the increase in cars and commercial vehicles will come from developing economies. According to the OPEC, road transportation accounts for over 40% of world oil consumption in 2006, and the demand is still on the rise.[232]

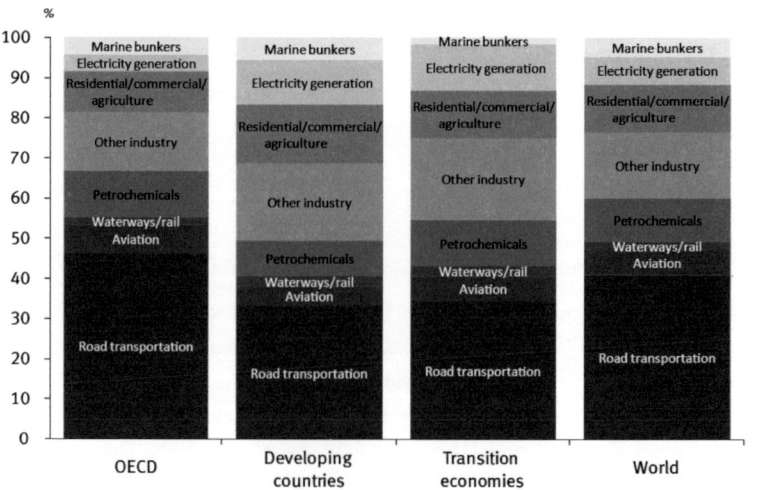

(Based on OPEC, OECD, IEA Energy Balances of OECD/ non. OECD 2008)

Figure 40: Distribution of oil demand accross sectors

---

[231] Cf. OPEC (2009), p. 88
[232] Cf. OPEC (2009), p.77

There are two important external risks for corporations. First, transportation costs and oil demand are directly linked with each other. An increase in demand leads to higher oil prices, and therefore the costs of transportation rise. The logical consequence is that supply chain costs of corporations, and transportation costs for car owner's rise, because of higher oil prices. Therefore, a rising demand for oil bears a risk for private and commercial customers in developed, as well as, in emerging economies. Moreover, depending on the demand, the oil price may rise to a level, which is harmful to the global economy. In this case, governmental regulations should regulate the oil markets, to reduce the influence of oil speculations on Brent and WTI futures.

Second, the depicted demand in the emerging countries will not only lead to a higher living standard for these countries, but also to a rise of carbon dioxide emissions. This will have a negative effect on the GET climate change. As a side note, for emerging economies no regulations on carbon dioxide emissions exist. For the EU, the recently adopted climate and energy legislative package involves a binding target of 120g CO_2/km, phased in over the period 2012–2015, with fines payable by manufacturers for not meeting these targets.[233]

Nevertheless, the climate conference in Copenhagen did not bring up an agreement for emerging economies.[234] This underscores the necessity to achieve political regulations on a global level. Western Governments have already urged the consumers to reduce energy consumption and to cut the dependence on imported oil. U.S. President Obama announced $3.4 billion in grants to boost the efficiency of the country's power-transmission network. As demand growth slows, the world may still face a supply crunch and surging prices as the recession crimps investment in new projects.[235]

4.1.1.2 Oil supply

As stated in chapter one by 2050, the supply of oil cannot support less than half the number of people in their present way of life.[236] The OPEC case study includes a projection for oil supply until the year 2030. It implicates that the rising demand especially by emerging economies may be supplied until the year 2030. This can be guaranteed by strong increase in non-crude supply from both OPEC and Non-OPEC sources, as depicted below.

---

[233] Cf. OPEC (2009), p. 99
[234] Cf. Economist (2009 j), p.24
[235] Cf. Bloomberg (2009)
[236] Eg. Campbell (2009)

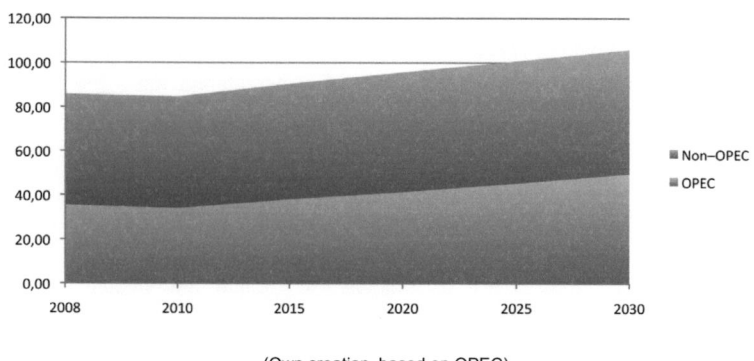

(Own creation, based on OPEC)

Figure 41: Supply by OPEC and other countries in mb / d[237]

There are three important takeaways from this case. First, according to the OPEC, the resources from crude oil together with non-crude oil are more than sufficient to meet the future demand until 2030. This projection is comparable to other projections from the energy Information Administration of the US Department of Energy (DOE/IEA) and the International Energy Agency (IEA).[238] Therefore, the economic growth until 2030 can be financed based on crude oil.

Second, the OPEC case study projects that the economic growth is constantly rising, according to their positive GDP assumptions, which leads to a constantly increasing demand for energy. This is a realistic foundation for the estimation of energy demand. Even if the economy has downturns in its future development, the demand is still feasible.

Third, renewable energy will play a bigger role in the future, even though it is estimated to grow on a low base.[239] In addition, today it is not clear which renewable energy will play another dominant role on the global energy market. However, oil will still play the central role as a primary energy source. Besides oil, nuclear energy and coal as primary energy source will also play a dominant role after 2030. This development depends strongly on technology aspects. If scientific research finds new or better solutions for energy production, the future energy mix may look different. Finding alternatives for transportation energy is the most important problem. In this regard, science has to provide a substitution for oil as the primary energy source.

---

[237] Cf. OPEC (2009), p.61
[238] Cf. OPEC (2009), p.75
[239] Cf. OPEC (2009), p. 39

4.1.1.3 Oil price volatility

The preceding analysis excluded an estimation of price development. "Oil price volatility in the recent past has been extreme."[240] This fact cannot be linked to the shortage of resources, even though that the OPEC tries to control the oil price by cutting back the production. As the following example shows, the annual average price of 2008, the price per barrel reached $ 91, whereas one year later, the annual average price was $ 43. Depicted below is the average annual development.

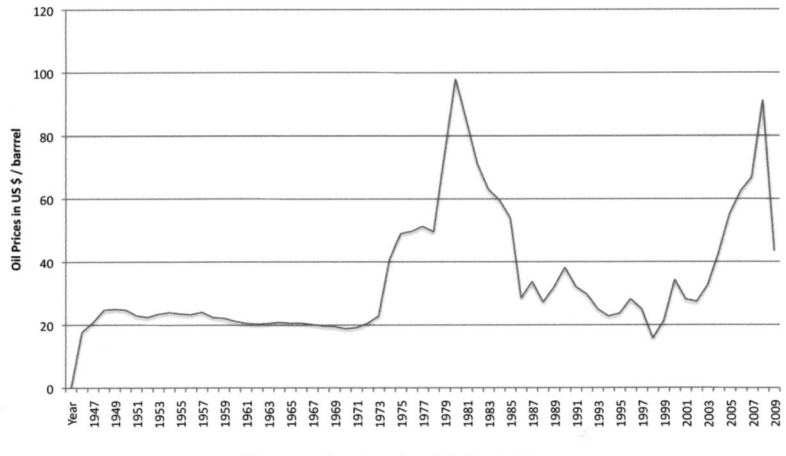

(Own creation, based on inflationdata)

Figure 42: Oil Price Development[241]

Concerning the daily trading activities, the oil price is even more volatile due to speculations. Depicted below is the average annual development. According to the OPEC, the emergence of oil as a financial asset class led to increased activity by non-commercials, with enhanced liquidity and volatility. In this respect, the paper oil market witnessed a transformation into an investment market, with prices exhibiting the characteristics of financial assets, rather than simply reflecting oil market fundamentals.[242] Therefore, it is most important that the oil price reflects the industry expansion, because a low oil price threatens industry wide investments.[243]

---

[240] Cf. OPEC (2009), p. 164
[241] Cf. Inflationdata (2009)
[242] Cf. OPEC (2009), p. 165
[243] Cf. OPEC (2009), p. 166

4.1.1.4 Final Risk assumptions

Based on the preceding analysis of the OPEC case study, and the preceding analysis in chapter one, the following external risks for the VC can be written down.

1. Rising Oil demand leads to higher fuel prices

2. Oil prices may be volatile, or reach new heights due to speculations

3. Binding target of Co2 [g] / km may cause the corporation to pay extra fees, if the targets are not met

4. Not enough supply of crude Oil after 2050 to support the existing business operations

5. These risks are affecting the company's portfolio, as well as, the strategic business units within the corporation. However, these external risks need to be qualified to appoint the internal risks that arise out of the risk assumption. Therefore, the next task within the GET assessment framework is to find out the possible threats to the overall risk to the corporate portfolio, as well as, which business operations in the strategic value chain are affected mostly.

4.1.2 Value chain evaluation

Oil price has an immediate effect on the development of fuel price. This direct effect has indirect consequences on production of goods and services, logistic processes, emissions, and environmental performance of corporations, as depicted below.[244]

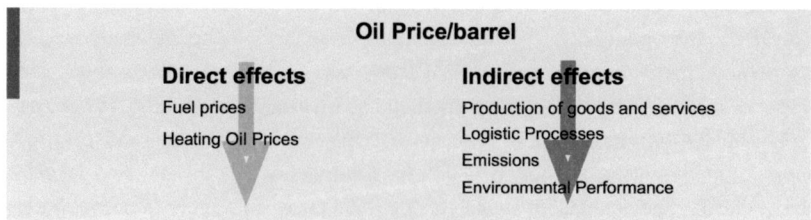

(Own creation)

Figure 43: Direct and indirect effects of the oil price development

Oil price development is the number one contributor to inflation and stagflation in leading economies. In the manufacturing industry, existing plants were replaced,

---

[244] Cf. Klepzig (2008), p. 20

because they were not efficient in the sense of oil consumption. Even more, the value of a certain production asset was even higher, when it did not depend on oil.[245] By this means, development of the oil/price has to be projected on the strategic value chain of the corporation. Even though, that processes along the SBUs may vary, it is possible to identify possible bottlenecks that are valid for the overall VC. In a real scenario, these bottlenecks need to be refined by the management of each of the SBUs. Latter is the step of quantification. By including the management of the SBU, this approach is called bottom-up approach, because estimation is not only done on the level of the corporation.

4.1.2.1 Impact to Achievement

4.1.2.1.1 Procurement

Due to the direct effects on oil prices, a rise of oil demand has an effect on the procurement process of the corporation. Especially the quality of preliminary products may suffer due to higher transportation costs, because stakeholders may reduce their product quality or increase prices to stay competitive. This has a direct impact on the switching costs. For example, if a manufacturer cannot stay competitive or even goes bankrupt because of transportation costs, the affected SBU needs to find new manufactures to meet their business goals. This may have a huge impact for the pharmaceutical industry, which audits their suppliers according to the good manufacturing standard (GMP) by the federal drug association (FDA). In this case, the switching costs may increase sharply.

4.1.2.1.2 Production

With an increase of oil prices, the production of the VC is affected in several ways. First, the cost structure of the product, or the cost of goods manufactured, increases, due to higher transportation costs. With higher production costs, the price for the product may need to be adopted, to meet the business requirements. In this case, a higher price may lead to a decrease in sales, depending on the competitor's position. Therefore, this development implicates cash flow volatility, because the sales are volatile. Second, with a sharp increase in prices, the costs of good manufactured may be extended to a point, where the product is not accepted by its customers, simply, because it is too expensive. Third, not only transportation costs, but also the overall manufacturing and supply chain costs are depended on the development of the oil price. This may lead to a shift of production to cheap labor countries (emerging economies), because the prices for

---

[245] Cf. Bishop (2009), p.231

manufacturing in a certain region management may need to re-plan their manufacturing strategy.

According to the product and industry, the supply of enough crude oil may lead to another internal production risk. Depending on the product, oil is used as a preliminary product, especially in the chemical, as well as, in the petrochemical industry. This has the consequence that without a supply of oil, the existing products cannot be manufactured or sold anymore. This leads directly to shutdown of the business operation, even if the product has been a star or a source of income in the corporate portfolio.

4.1.2.1.3 Sales

In regard of sales process, the oil price has a direct effect on the product quality, the price margin, and the market share of the product. First, as depicted in the preceding paragraph, a rising oil price may harm the suppliers within the total value chain of the corporation. This may lead to a quality reduction of preliminary products, and therefore will cause a quality reduction of the VC products. Second, a high oil price also causes higher value chain costs. If no measures are applied, to optimize the value chain costs, the price margin decreases. This will automatically cause effects on the market share.

4.1.2.1.4 Personal

The effect of oil price and personal may not be evident, but an increase of the oil price bears also a risks for companies that do not try to reduce the consumption of oil, to meet their business requirements, and tend for other measures like reducing the product quality. Environmental friendly operations of a corporation, product quality, as well as, corporate social responsibility measures are not only positive in the sense of external marketing, but as well as, on the internal marketing. Especially companies who operate environmental friendly and try to reduce the capacity of CO_2 consumed have a positive marketing effect. In this case, personal is more motivated to work at a company that strongly respects the environment.

4.1.2.1.5 Capital

In the sense of strategic value chain analysis, capital refers to capital that is directly needed to support the production process. Therefore, oil price directly affects the cash flow that is needed to support business processes. The financial resources of the stakeholders may also be at risk, depending on the value configuration of the company. Depending on the financial situation, companies must take further debts, because they need to finance need machinery that meet regulatory means, that are more efficient in the sense of oil consumption, or in the worst case, they need to shift their production facilities to low labor cost countries. In all cases, the oil price has an affect on the debt equity ratio of the company.

4.1.2.2 Impact to administration

4.1.2.2.1 Business Planning

There are three takeaways on how the four external risks affect corporate development and strategic business planning of the SBUs. First, a high volatility of oil price means a high volatility of transportation costs, and supply chain costs, as well as, a high volatility on the generated cash flow. This may lead to a quality reduction of business planning, because business goals may not be set valid. Second, binding targets for CO_2 emissions are growth hurdles, if a corporation lacks environmental measures. Especially in emerging economies, these measures are perceived as political chains that hinder corporation in growing, because the environmental standards are not set yet. Third, existing corporations that are strongly depended on oil and have a growth target that reaches beyond 2050, must develop measures on how to become more independent from crude oil. Especially in the transportation industry, as well as, in petrochemical industry alternatives to oil as a primary energy source, or as a preliminary product, need to be implemented.

4.1.2.2.2 Controlling

The quality of controlling in the sense of controlling systems, and coordination of controlling in corporations is also affected by the external oil risks. Controllers, especially risk controllers, are mostly affected by oil price development. They need to carefully analyze the development of the oil price by monitoring directly, or with the help of monitoring software, to carefully distinct between market noise and real trend. Besides external risk allocation, controllers must also analyze the internal development of the portfolio concerning the risks.

4.1.2.2.3 Corporate Culture

The whole culture of the corporation is also affected by the oil price risk. Ideally, the innovative capacity of the corporate culture helps to find new solutions against risks. However, corporate leaders have to ensure that possible risks do not have a negative effect on the productivity of the corporation. In this case, effective communication of strategy reduces uncertainty of the workforce.

4.1.2.3 Concluding quantification of risks

After the internal risks have been qualified with the value chain analysis, it is time to quantify the risks according to urgency and importance, to determine possible emergency measure for short-term reactions, and preemptive measures that can be applied to assure the long-term survival of the SBU.

	Urgency	Importance
1. Procurement		
1.1. Lack of Quality of preliminary products	⊖	+
1.2. Switching Costs	⊖	+
2. Production		
2.1. Manufacturing Costs	⊖	+
2.2. Supply Chain Costs	⊖	+
2.3. Substitute Products	⊖	+
2.4. Product Quality	⊖	+
3. Sales		
3.1. Product Quality	⊖	⊖
3.2. Price Margin	⊖	+
3.3. Market Share	⊖	+
4. Personal		
4.1 Identification with the Corporation	⊖	⊖
5. Capital		
5.1. Own financial resources	+	+
5.2. Financial Resources of stakeholders	⊖	+
6. Business Development		
6.1. Quality of business planning	⊖	⊖
6.2. Binding targets	⊖	⊖
7. Controlling		
7.1. Risk controlling	⊖	⊖
7.2. IT infrastructure	⊖	⊖
8. Corporate Culture	⊖	⊖

(Own creation)

Figure 44: Urgency and Importance evaluation by a SBU of the VC

Above figure visualizes an assessment questionnaire that has been filled out by a strategic business unit within the VC that produces a chemical product that preliminary products are fully based on oil derivates. The management of the SBU quantifies the internal risks that have been found through the value chain analysis. This questionnaire should ideally be implemented within the knowledge management system of the corporation. Based on this information, corporate management has now more detailed information available on how the GET is affecting the SBU. Based on this information, possible portfolio measures can be implemented with more precision, and possible wrong decisions are avoided.

4.1.3   Financial evaluation

Based on the concepts introduced in chapter three, the management of the VC, as well as, the management of the SBUs within the corporate environment must ensure that liquidity is guaranteed to support the business operations. In this case, current assets and current liabilities are at the heart of the financial evaluation, in other words the working capital. This measure is valid, because the SBU has a production unit. For a service unit, this measure is not applicable, because the amount of assets is not sufficient for efficient working capital measures.

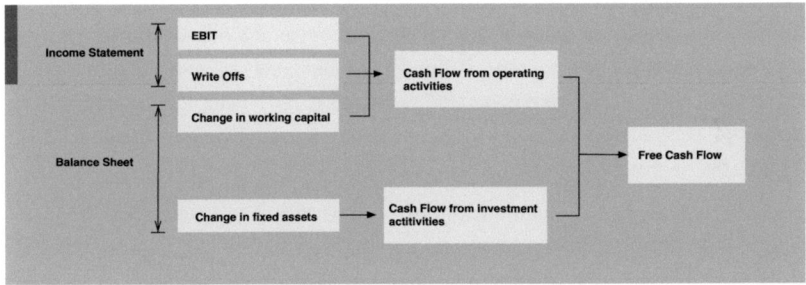

(Own creation, based on Klepzig)

Figure 45: The influence of working capital on liquidity[246]

Depicted above, there is a strong connection between working capital and liquidity. A reduction of working capital influences those assets related to the balance sheet. Consequently, the costs of capital are reduced, which leads to a better economic value added (EVA).[247]

As the preceding analysis showed, a high volatility of the oil price, leads to a high volatility of cash flow, in the wider sense. In the narrower sense, the cash flow from operating activities is negatively impacted. Therefore, those assets that have the strongest relation to oil price, for example oil reserves, or manufacturing equipment, needs to be monitored closely.

In this regard, working capital management is a core component in value management, especially in assuring company risks to cash flow volatilities. Concerning the assessment framework for GETs, working capital measures are referred as emergency measures, as well as, constant measures that need to be applied to stabilize cash flow volatilities within the corporation, and to ensure liquidity.

---

[246] Cf. Klepzig (2008), p.19
[247] Cf. Klepzig (2008), p.18

4.2   Implementation of measures

The assessment framework delivers threats to the overall corporation, as well as, to specific SBUs within the company. The final step is now to conquer these risks by finding and establishing countermeasures for the overall corporation, and the SBUs to fine-tune the strategic levers for portfolio management.

The countermeasures are related to time. In case of urgent threats, emergency measures should be applied. Short-term and long-term countermeasures address the targets for the related change management program.

The strategic measures goals be formulated and implemented into the company's knowledge management system. If the corporation has its own intranet portal, then these goals can be communicated more easily, to ensure that all employees within the cooperation have an idea on where the company is heading. This reduces the degree of uncertainty, and raise the quality of planning.

In a cyclic period, the achievement of these goals needs to be monitored. This can be achieved with benchmarking via questionnaires, and by personal-to-personal interviews.[248] It must be stated here, that a realistic implementation of change measures requires a detailed specification of the business environment, the value configuration, the product, and the market situation. Even though, there is enough evidence at hand to show what measures are possible for a chemical company.

4.2.1 Emergency measures

As a rule of thumb, in times of crisis liquidity is more important over return on invest. Cash flow is therefore more important than company value.[249] Not only is the income and loss statement of the organization affected, more over processes within the production, suppliers, customers, and people are affected as well. A possible cause for a rise of the oil price in 2010 has been identified. There is the chance that oil prices will reach unforeseen summits. In memory, the SBU of the VC has valuated the risk own financial resources as urgent and important.

Based on this assumption, the following strategic levers were identified to ensure the business operation of the SBU. Depicted below is a set of six countermeasures, or strategic levers, which can be applied to protect the competitive position of the corporation if necessary. These measures may be applied if the business is harmed by the actual economic development.

---

[248] Cf. Platt (2004)
[249] Cf. Klepzig (2008), p. 15

No	Countermeasure	Strategic Level
1	Liquidation of non profitable financial assets	Corporate
2	Divest unnecessary asset of working capital	SBU, Department
3	Reduce the business trips	All
4	Raise productivity	All
5	Optimize Cost Structure	All, especially SBU
6	Optimize human resource structure	All

Table 4: Emergency measures

Depending of the financial portfolio of the corporation, financial assets may be sold. This money can be gained easily, because the financial transaction of equities can be processed within a day. The gained money can be invested directly into business operations of SBUs.

Working assets that are used for manufacturing operations may also be sold to optimize the working capital structure. It must be stated here that working capital optimization may not be possible if the SBU is only running service operations. This measure can be applied within a short timeframe, depending on the significance of the asset.

Companies that operate on a global level may reduce their spending on business trips to save money. Besides the saving of money, less energy is consumed and CO_2 production is reduced. This measure can be applied on all levels.

Productivity is defined as the ration effort to success. To raise the productivity, which is directly to earnings, the effort can be raised. Therefore, the productivity is raised directly and more profit can be gained.

Another lever is to optimize the cost structure. This is based on an identification of potential cost drivers that are not influencing the production processes directly. If potential cost positions are identified, then these can be liquidated. Furthermore, if the SBU is producing more than one product, then a valid measure would also be to concentrate the production effort to the most valuable product,

The last lever that can be applied is to optimize the human resource structure. Even though, this measure should only be applied if no other options are available, because it means a reduction of human and knowledge capital. To avoid a loss of human capital, short-time work during the time of crisis can help to avoid the dismissal of workforce.

4.2.2 Change management program

As a starting point for the planning of the structural change management program, the long-term goals and the short-term goals for the change need to be identified. These goals are the strategic levers for the corporate strategy and define the direction for the change. Long-term goals define the baseline for the business transformation and are closely related to the overall vision and strategy. Short-term goals are the quick wins of the overall program that need to be established quickly to gain the acceptance, and to empower broad based action.

With the defined goals, the framework of the change management program is drawn. Concerning the corporate evaluation, the planning range should begin in 2010 and reaches until 2030.

The change management program has to consider procurement, production, capital, as well as, supply of resources to fully tackle the risks that arise out of the scarcity scenario. There are changes that need to done on the level of the corporation, as well as, on the level of SBUs. Scarcity of oil is affecting the overall cooperation. Therefore, all levels of the organization should be integrated into the program, and a responsible person of each levels of the organization should be part of the guiding coalition. Knowledge management measures accompany the process and help to coordinate the overall change, as well as, to refine the change measures that are applied. As discussed in the preceding chapters, the approach of the GET assessment framework strongly suggests this measure to raise the overall efficiency of change.

4.2.2.1 Long term goals

As depicted in the risk analysis, there is a strong possibility that the supply of oil may be very scarce after 2030. This leads to the fact that only half of the humanity may hold up their economic standard based on cheap oil. On the industrial level, especially corporations in the chemical and in the transportation sector will suffer. In the figure "distribution of oil demand across sectors", this is evident, as transportation is the main consumer of oil, followed by the chemical industry.

Long-term goals lay the baseline, or stay as a beacon, for the overall change process. Short-term goals are aligned to these long-term goals, and can be perceived as the first milestones that need to be reached in order to guarantee a success to the overall change effort.

Due to the scarcity of oil supply, this paper suggests that companies will have to pursue a mix of the following three options to support their business operations in the long-term.

No	Countermeasure	Strategic Level
1	Find substitution for oil	SBU
2	Divest unnecessary asset of working capital	SBU, Department
3	Ensure the supply of oil	All

Table 5: Long-term targets for the change management program

First, a substitution for oil needs to be found that replace either production materials, or serve as an alternative fuel. Especially in the chemical industry, oil is used for the production of 80 percent of the preliminary materials. The core element that is used for the synthesis of these preliminary products is carbon, which is also enclosed in natural gas, and in carbon dioxide. Even though, today is chemical supply chain is optimized for the usage of oil.

Therefore, enormous investments are needed to enhance the chemical reaction processes for the production of chemical materials based on natural gas, or based on carbon dioxide.[250] At his point, basic research is still necessary to bridge the divide between theoretical approaches and practical application. Especially the usage of carbon dioxide for the production of preliminary products is still in its infancy. This goal can be perceived as an overall goal for the chemical industry. In this case, the overall industry, as well as, research institutes need to be incorporated into the process of finding alternatives. Even more, if materials based on an oil substitution are used within the production, then several assets need to be divested, because they will become useless in the future. In this regard, working capital measures supplement the effort of finding and implementing alternative processes. Therefore, working capital optimization is a steady process that complements the actual change operations.

In conclusion, this option is a future scenario that may seem to be far away. Even though, corporations should prepare themselves for this scenario today. This can be done step by step. A starting point for all corporations within the chemical industry is to be strongly involved in scientific research. In the best case, this enables corporations to integrate possible breakthroughs early into their production, which is a direct competitive advantage.[251] In the worst case, companies do not invest into options that may not be applicable on an industrial scale. In all cases, corporations can estimate the possible outcome of scientific findings on a very early stage. In case of alternative to fuel, three options are

---

[250] Cf. Hoffmann (2010)
[251] Cf. Porter (2002), pp. 220

possible in the near future. Alternative a may be electrical energy, alternative b may be other fuels like biodiesel, and alternative c is the fuel cell.

The main problem in case of (a) is the storage of electrical energy in vehicles. Today's concept of batteries does not provide the necessary capacity to replace the existing storage concept of a tank. Researchers and startup companies compete for the best technology that is capable to store enough electrical energy. Still, research time is needed. Alternative (b) has a major drawback, because crops are needed for the production of biofuels. Due to the rising population of the world, more area under cultivation is needed to meet the supply of food. In this case, there is a mutually dependence between crops and fuels. From the macro economical point of view, this is a prisoner's dilemma. The fuel cell, alternative (c), is an electrochemical device which converts free energy of a chemical reaction into electrical energy, mostly based on methanol or hydrogen. The major drawback is the generation of hydrogen is the electrolysis processes needed for production.[252]

All alternatives have the problem that the necessary infrastructure needs to be deployed in order to use the technology most efficiently. Today, there is no infrastructure available in the western economies that support the supply of alternative energy sources on a broad base. Even though, there is an exception to the rule. Japan is the strongly investing into new technologies based on electricity. The Japanese government is building electricity fuel stations where electric fueled cars can be refueled. This is done in corporation with Nissan, and a company called better place.[253]

Besides finding substitution materials and alternative energy, companies need to ensure that hold stake at the oil supply in the near future. Again, this is important for all industries, where oil plays an important role within the value chain, like chemical and transportation companies. In this case, companies can gain their own access to the oil markets, as well as, to strive for cooperation with partners that hold their own access to markets.[254] In the former case, companies can build up their own reserves of oil within their supply chain. In this case, huge investments need to be done, in order to achieve a sustainable capacity to support the business operations. For most companies building their own resources of oil is not an efficient option.

---

[252] Basu (2007), p.53
[253] Cf. Focus (2009)
[254] Cf. Börsenzeitung (2009), p.2

4.2.2.2 Short term goals

Short-term goals, or quick wins, are targets that should be reached within two years. In terms of scarcity of resources, several quick wins may be reached from the beginning of 2010 until 2012. Again a set of different levers has been identified that can be applied to fully conquer the risk. All measures should be applied at the same time, to empower broad based action.

No	Countermeasure	Strategic Level
1	Reduce the fuel consumption of the vehicle fleet	All
2	Invest into better IT technology	All
3	Optimize working capital	All, especially SBU

Table 6: Quick wins for the change program

To reduce the consumption of fuel, technology plays a key role. Depending on the efficiency of the vehicle fleet, there may be vehicles that consume more fuel than other vehicles, because they run on old technology. The best option until 2012 is to upgrade existing vehicles with modern technology like eco tuning, low weight tires, or better machine oils. In each of these cases, the consumption of oil may be reduced between 0.2 and 2.0 liters per 100 kilometers. Another option is also to divest old cars, and to invest into modern vehicles that already consume less oil based fuels. Depending on the size of the vehicle fleet this will bring an enormous reduction.

An investment into better IT Technology has certain benefits. First, better IT means more and better options for conference calls, for example with the use of webcams in combination with software technology. Managers within the company can hold meetings as if they sit together within a meeting room. Second, by this means, the fuel consumption is reduced, because travel expenses are reduced. This leads to a better efficiency of oil consumption. Furthermore, an investment into green IT also reduces the consumption of electricity.

Working capital measures on all levels of the corporation, especially on the SBU level, needs to complement the optimization measures. In case of investments into modern technology that reduce the consumption of fuel, working capital measures ensure that the remaining technology is divested. In conclusion, for producing companies working capital is by far the most important lever to ensure the liquidity needed to support the business operations.

5   Conclusion and outlook

In conclusion, scientific findings that arise out of the analysis of the impact of Global Economic Trends and their impact to Corporate Development are manifold. The bottom line of this thesis is that the methodologies of risk analysis and change management need to be incorporated into the strategic planning process of corporate development to fully identify and to tackle the risks. By this means, the possible internal risks can be identified, and necessary counter measures can be developed and implemented with the methodologies of change management.

The top seven Global Economic Trends, which have been revealed in chapter one, deliver a basis for risk analysis, as required. As shown, these trends drive today's markets to new secular destination, and impact corporations. Even though, the analysis is limited here, because the overall overview of the certain trends is not sufficient for detailed business planning. The strategic management of the corporation needs to dive deeper into the context of the given trends, to determine the real risk to the corporate portfolio. The approach on how to dive deeper into the context was shown within the case study.

Chapter 2 delivered the necessary methodologies to determine the impact to corporations, in the sense of corporate strategy, business planning, portfolio management, and value based management. As a result, existing methods do encounter risk, but refinement and new methodologies to describe the complexity of modern markets are needed. The hypothesis of this paper is, that existing mathematical methods need to be refined with profound risk analysis to reduce the portfolio risk to an absolute minimum. Even though, the finding of this paper is that existing models, like the portfolio theory, are still valid, but in times of market inconsistencies, better models are needed to describe the more complex environment, like the approaches of behavioral finance, or the methodologies of working capital. Therefore, risk management of corporations should pursue both mathematically risk diversification, as well as, qualitative risk assessment. Furthermore, in a complex corporate environment, the degree of risk concerning a specific GET may vary across the overall business, because SBUs may operate in different markets. Consequently, risk assessment should be incorporated into the strategic business planning. Due to this, the true impact to the corporation can be determined, and countermeasures can be integrated into the business planning.

In Chapter 2.5.1, the study of an A.T. Kirney provided insights about reasons for bankruptcy. Wrong and late or not consequent decision-making is among the top reasons why business fail. Especially in turbulent time, when markets tend to react volatile, information plays a key role for effective management.

Based on these findings, the core framework of this thesis, the GET assessment framework, has been developed. It incorporates both the identification of risks and the implementation of strategic measures. Its main intent is to provide a standardized way on how to access risks that are related to Global Economic Trends.

The framework may be beneficial for all strategic levels of the corporations, because it reflects the potential risks to corporations concerning strategic levels of the company from top to down. This model is especially beneficial for broad diversified MNCs, where the businesses of each SBU vary. In this case, the model helps to reflect if a GET has a certain risk to a specific part of the value chain. In other words, the external risk is projected to the corporation to determine the internal risk. By this means, the quality of business planning on the corporate level is raised, because the strategic management on all levels is able to pinpoint potential bottlenecks. It must be stated here that even managers that do not have a background in economics can participate directly in the assessment. This also enhances the quality of risk assessment, because the view on the risk is more detailed and more knowledge is gained.

Due to the integration of knowledge management practices, the framework has even more benefits. First, decision makers on all levels within the corporate environment are integrated directly into the strategic change process. Due to this, the awareness of certain risks is raised. Second, knowledge that has been gained during the change process can be integrated more easily into the corporate culture, which automatically raises the efficiency of change and strategic decision-making. By this means, information about certain risks is manifested into the roots of business management. This information can be refined during over time. This also leads to the fact that the development of a change process can be monitored more effectively. In summary, the efficiency of strategic planning is raised.

To prove the applicability of the framework the case study has shown how the model can be adopted to access the potential risks to a corporation that operates within the chemical industry. Because the corporation is a virtual corporation, some limitations were encountered. On the one hand, there are no facts available about the value configuration of the corporation. On the other hand, no numbers about the operational performance of the business were available. Therefore, a real implementation of these measures could not be shown directly. Even though, the application of the assessment framework has been shown on the corporate level, as well as, on the level of the SBU. By taking a closer look at the virtual business processes of the SBU, potential internal risks could be manifested. Results of the assessment were emergency measures and countermeasures for the short-term, and the long-term planning of change projects. These goals are sufficient to give direction for the future business development. Hence, the limitation is not critical for the valuation, and covers the relevant aspects about changes within the chemical industry, which are evoked by the scarcity scenario. Overall, the applicability of the GET framework was proven.

To conclude, as markets tend to react more volatile, and stability will become a luxury, new methodologies are needed to incorporate trends, and to enhance risk management. The approach of this paper was to give the reader a holistic view on Global Economic Trends and on how to integrate the associated risks to Corporate Development. Further research should concentrate on the refinement and enhancement of the tools that were applied within the framework. Especially, the methodologies that were suggested within chapter 2.5.1 should be enhanced. This can be accomplished by delegating the three elements of the corporate evaluation to respective academic experts. Furthermore, experts within the field of information technology should accompany the process to give guidance for the application of knowledge management tools. By this means, the techniques used are improved, which leads to an overall enhancement of the quality of the approach. This should be an iterative process in order to integrate new academic research findings. MNCs can apply this framework with minor enhancements, because experts from of controlling, engineering, and strategic management are available, or can be provided from partner companies. There are two constraints to the application. First, the described process of knowledge exchange needs to be integrated into an existing knowledge management system, or an IT System needs to be established that is capable to run the described business process. To give the reader an idea, an ERP System like SAP can be used for this process, as well as, a third party system that has just the purpose of knowledge management. Even though, each of these systems has to be customized in order to fit into the corporate IT landscape. Second, the overall process is a change to existing processes within the corporation. Therefore, it should be integrated by applying the methodologies of change management. A management directive alone may not be sufficient to establish the desired process of knowledge exchange. If the process will be established, corporations are less resistant to the associated risk of GETs, and they have a competitive advantage.

Bibliography

A.T. Kearney, 2009. Nachhaltige Restrukturierung [online]. ATKearney.de. Available from: http://www.atkearney.de/content/veroeffentlichungen/whitepaper_detail.php/id/507 95/practice/strat_strategie [Accessed 11 December 2009]

Antil, N. and Lee, K., 2008. Company Valuation Under IFRS: Interpreting and Forecasting Accounts Using. 2nd edition, Hampshire: Hariman House:

Aswathappa, K., 2008. International Business. New Delhi: Tata MC-Graw Hill

Awad, E. and M., Ghaziri, H. M., 2005. Knowledge Management. 2nd edition. New Delhi: Dorling Kindersley

Basu, S., 2007. Recent Trends in Fuel Cell Science and Technolgy. New York: Springer

Baumöl, U., 2008. Change Management in Organisationen. Wiesbaden: Gabler

BEA, F. X. and Haas, J., 2001, Strategisches Management. 4th edition. Stuttgart: Lucius&Lucius

Bishop, M., 2009. Economics: An A-Z Guide. London: The Economist

Börsenzeitung, 2009. Bayer will Rohstoffbezug dauerhaft sichern. Frankfurt am Main: Wertpapier-Mitteilungen Keppler

Boston Consulting Group, 2006. On Strategy: Classic Concepts and New Perspectives. New Jersey: John Wiley & Sons

Brealey, R. A. and Meyers, S., 2003. Principles of Corporate Finance. 7th edition. New York: MC-Graw-Hill

Bress, S., 2007. Corporate Governance in Deutschland. Troisdorf: EUL Verlag

Buchholtz, U., 2006. Megatrend Rohstoffe: Chancen, Risiken, Perspektiven, Empfehlungen. Berlin: Fuchsbriefe

Bukowitz, W. R. and Williams, R. L., 1999. The Knowledge Management Fieldbook. London: Pearson Education

Business Dictionary, 2010. Definition of a trend [online]. Business Dictionary.com.Available from: http://www.businessdictionary.com/definition/trend.html [Accessed 4 February 2010]

Button, C. J., 1980. Economics and Corporate Strategy. New York: Cambridge University Press

Cameron, E. and Green, M., 2004. Making sense of change management: a complete guide to the models, tools. London: Kogan Page

Campbell, J. C., 2009. Key oil figures were distorted by US pressure, says whistleblower [online]. PeakOil.net. Available from: http://www.peakoil.net/files/Campbell_comments_20091110.pdf [Accessed 5 February 2010]

Canadell J.G., Dickson R., Hibbard K., Raupach M. and Young O., 2003. Global Carbon Project Report No. 1 [online]. Globalcarbonproject.com. Available from: http://www.globalcarbonproject.org/science/sfi.htm [Accessed 5 February 2010]

Carlesi, L., Verster, B. and Wegner, F., 2007. Perspective on Corporate Finance and Strategy. McKinsey Quaterly [online], 23. Available from: https://www.mckinseyquarterly.com/article_print.aspx?L2=5&L3=2&ar=1965 [Accessed 5 February 2010]

Cohen, S. D. and Kotter, J., 2002. The heart of change. Boston: Harvard Business School Press

Colley, J. L., Doyle, J. C. and Hardie, R. D., 2004. Corporate Strategy: How to restructure a business unit to best support corporate goals, New York: Mc-Graw Hill

Crainer, S. and Dearlove, D., 2004. Financial Times Handbook of Management, 3rd edition. London: Pearson Education

De Bondt, W.F.M. and Thaler, R.H., 1985. Does the stock market overreact? Journal of Finance, 793-805. Berkeley: The American Finance Association

Dess, G. G., 2004. Strategic Management: Creating Competitive Advantages, 2nd edition. New York: Mc-Graw Hill

Doppler, K. and Lauterburg, C., 2005. Change Management den Unternehmenswandel gestalten, 11th edition. Frankfurt: Campus Verlag

Doty, S. and Turner, C., 2009. Energy Management Handbook, 7th edition. Lilburn: The Fairmont Press

Drucker, P., 2007. Management Challenges for the 21st century. Oxford: Elsevier

El-Erian, M., 2008. When markets collide, New York: MC-Graw Hill

Ernst & Young, 2009. What is next for Corporate Development? [online]. EY.com. Available from: http://www.ey.com/AT/de/Services/Transactions/Corporate-Development [Accessed 29 November 2009]

Ernst&Young, 2010. Corporate Development [online]. EY.com. Available from: http://www.ey.com/DE/de/Services/Transactions/Corporate-Development [Accessed 4 February 2010]

European Energy Commission, 2009. Investing in the Development of Low
Carbon Technologies. Brussels: Commission of the European Communities

Fabozzi, F. J., 1998. Handbook Portfolio Management, Pennsylvania: New Hope

Focus, 2009. Neuartige Elektroauto-Tankstelle vorgestellt, Offenburg: Burda
GmbH

Friedlob, G. T. and Welton, R. E., 2008. Keys to reading an annual report, 4th
edition. New York: Barron's Education

Gapminder, 2010. Total fertility [online]. Gapminder.com. Available from:
http://graphs.gapminder.org/world [Accessed 4 February 2010]

Gibson, R. C., 2000. Asset Allocation: Balancing Financial Risk, 3rd edition. New
York: McGraw Hill

Global Carbon Project, 2009. Carbon Budget 2008 [online].
Globalcarbonproject.com. Available from:
http://www.globalcarbonproject.org/carbonbudget/ [Accessed 5 February 2010]

Global Warming, 2010. Extracts from the IPCC 4th Report Summary for
policymakers [online]. Global-GreenHouse-Warming.com. Available from:
http://www.global-greenhouse-warming.com/IPCC-4th-Report-The-Physical-
Science-Basis.html [Accessed 6 February 2010]

Grant, R., 2005. Contemporary Strategy Analysis, 5th edition. Malden: Blackwell
Publishing

Groten, H. and Keuper, F., 2007. Nachhaltiges Change Management –
Interdisziplinäre Fallbeispiele und Perspektive. Wiesbaden: Gabler

Grüning, R. and Kühn, R., 2008. Process-based strategic planning, 5th edition.
Heidelberg: Springer

Hahn, D. and Taylor, B., 2005. Strategische Unternehmensführung, 9th edition. Berlin: Springer

Hammerschmidt, M., 2006. Marketing Performance. Wiesbaden: Gabler

Harvard Business Review, 1998. On Change. Boston: Harvard Business School Press

Harvard Business School, 2005. The essentials of managing change and transition. Boston: Harvard Business School Publishing

Hoffmann, S., 2010. Chemiebranche sucht nach Ölersatz [online]. Handelsblatt.de. Available from: http://www.handelsblatt.com/technologie/energie-umwelt/_b=2512501,_p=133,_t=ftprint,doc_page=0;printpage [Accessed 5 February 2010]

Inflation Data, 2009. Historical Crude Oil Prices [online]. Inflationdata.com. Available from: http://www.inflationdata.com/inflation/Inflation_Rate [Accessed 3 January 2010]

Intergovernmental Panel on Climate Change, 2007. Climate Change 2007: The physical science basis. Cambridge: Cambridge University Press

International Energy Agency, 2010. Oil Market Report [online]. IEA.org. Available from: http://omrpublic.iea.org/currentissues/full.pdf [Accessed 5 February 2010]

International Monetary Fund, 2009. World Economic Outlook. Washington: International Monetary Fund

Investopedia, 2010. Definition of market noise [online]. Investopedia.com. Available from: http://www.investopedia.com/terms/n/noise.asp [Accessed 5 February 2010]

Investorword, 2010. Definition OPEC [online]. Investorwords.com. Available from: http://www.investorwords.com/3431/OPEC.html [Accessed 5 February 20010]

Kaplan, R. S. and Norton, D. P., 1996. Balanced Scorecard, Boston: Harvard Business Press

Karalay, G. N., 2005. Integrated Approach to rural development, New Delhi: Concept Publishing

Kim, W. C. and Mauborgne, R., 2005. Blue Ocean Strategy. Harvard Business School Press: Boston

Klepzig, H. J., 2008. Working Capital und Cash Flow – Finanzströme durch Prozessmanagement optimieren. Wiesbaden: Gabler

Kostka, C. and Mönch, A., 2009. Change Management, 4th edition. München: Hanser Verlag

Kotter, J. P., 1999. On what leaders really do, Boston: Harvard Business School Press

Kotter, J. P., 2002. Leading Change. Boston: Harvard Business School Press

Kraus, M., 2008. OPEC-Die Geschichte einer Weltmacht [online]. Investor-Verlag.de. Available from: http://www.investor-verlag.de/opec-die-geschichte-einer-weltmacht-/111020542/ [Accessed 5 February 2010]

Kutschker, M. and Schmid, S., 2006. Internationales Management. München: Oldenbourg Verlag

Kwiatkowski, A. and Graham, R., 2009. IEA Cuts Global Demand Forecast on Economy [online]. Bloomberg.com. Available from: http://www.bloomberg.com/apps/news?pid=20601072 [Accessed 2 January 2010]

Leontiades, J., 1985. Multinational Corporate Strategy: Planning for World Markets. New York: The free press

Lipschutz, R. D. and Rowe, J. K., 2005. Globalization, Governmentality and Global Politics. New York: Routledge

Lobnig, H., Schwendenwein, J. and Zvacek, L., 2003. Beratung in der Veränderung: Grundlagen, Konzepte und Beispiele. Wiesbaden: Gabler

Locher, D., 2008. Value Stream Mapping for Lean Development. New York: Productivity Press

Lohnes, G. R., 2008. Energy costs drive sustainability [online]. Ugl-Unicco.com. Available from: http://www.ugl-unicco.com/downloads/news-events/unicco-in-print/0208EnergyCost_Reprint.pdf [Accessed 5 February 2010]

Maginn, J. L., 2007. Managing investment portfolios: a dynamic process, 3rd edition. CFA Institue. New Jersey: Wiley & Sons

Mankiw, N. G., 2008. Principles of Macroeconomics, 5th edition. Mason: Cengage Learning

Mattli, W. and Woods, N., 2009. The Politics of Global Regulation. New Jersey: Princeton University Press

McKinsey, 2007. The New power brokers: How Oil, Asia, Hedge Funds, and Private Equity Are shaping Global Capital Markets. San Francisco: McKinsey Global Institute

McKinsey, 2009. Global Capital Market: Entering a new Era. San Francisco: McKinsey Global Institute

Meyer, C. A., 2007. Working Capital und Unternehmenswert. Wiesbaden: Gabler

Naisbitt, J., 1988. Megatrends – Ten New Directions Transforming Our Lives. New York: Grand Central Publishing

Nilakant, V. and Ramnarayan, 2007. Change management: Altering mindsets in a global context. New Delhi: Sage Publications

Oliver Wyman, 2007. Corporate Portfolio Management [online]. Oliverwyman.com. Available from: http://www.oliverwyman.com/fr/pdf_files/corp_portfolio_manage_ERC_0307.pdf [Accessed 21 December 2009]

OPEC, 2006. Long-Term Strategy. Wien: OPEC

OPEC, 2009. World Oil Outlook 2009. Wien: OPEC

Peak Oil Forum, 2010. Das Ende des billigen Öls und die Konsequenzen für die Gesellschaft [online]. PeakOilForum.de. Available from: http://www.peak-oil-forum.de/ [Accessed 5 February 2010]

Platt, N., 2004. Features – Change Strategies are the key to KM [online]. LLRX.com. Available from: http://www.llrx.com/node/40/print [Accessed 5 February 2010]

Pompian, M. M., 2006. Behavioral Finance and Wealth Management. New Jersey: John Wiley & Sons

Porter, M. E., 1998. On Competition: Updated and Expanded Edition, 4th edition. Boston: Harvard Business School Publishing

Prahalad, C. K. and Krishnan, M. S., 2008. The new age of innovation. New York: Mc-Graw Hill

Price, R. W., 2004. Roadmap to entrepreneurial success: Powerful strategies for Building a High-Profit Business. New York: Amacom

Quinn, R. E., 2004. Building the Bridge as you walk upon it, New Jersey: John Wiley &Sons

Riley, G., 2009. Revision: GDP and GNP [online]. Tutor2u. Available from:http://www.tutor2u.net/blog/index.php/economics/print/revision-gdp-and-gnp/ [Accessed 4 February 2010]

Robin, J. and Gillies, G. L., 1996. Global Business Strategy, London: Thomson Learning

Roland Berger, 2010. On Corporate Development [online]. Roland Berger. Available from:
http://www.rolandberger.com/expertise/functional_issues/strategy_and_corporate_excellence/strategic_planning/index.html [Accessed 6 Feburary 2010]

Rolfes, B., 2003. Moderne Investitionsrechnung, 3rd edition. München: Oldenbourg

Rothenbücher, J. and Schrottke, J., 2009. Nachhaltige Restrukturierung [online]. ATKirney.ch, Available from:
http://www.atkearney.ch/download/EB_21_Nachhaltige_Restrukturierung.pdf [Accessed 5 February 2010]

Rust, H., 2008. Zukunftsillusionen: Kritik der Trendforschung. Wiesbaden: VS Verlag

Scarlett, R., 2001. Value Based Management, 2nd edition. London: Cima

Scheuss, R., 2007. Handbuch der Strategien. Frankfurt: Campus Verlag

Schweikart, N. and Töpfer, A., 2006. Wertorientiertes Management, Berlin: Springer

Smit, P.J., 2007. Strategy Implementation Readings. Lansdowne: Juta&Co

Smith, G., 2004. Transforming Change – Manage Change, Compete & Win , 2nd edition. London: Kogan-Page

Smith, M., 2005. Performance Measurement & Management. London: Sage

Spreemann, K., 2006. Portfolio Management, 3rd edition. Wiesbaden: Oldenbourg

Spremann, K, 2006. Portfoliomanagement, 3rd edition. München: Oldenbourg

Steiner, M. and Bruns, C., 2007. Wertpapiermanagement – Professionelle Wertpapieranalyse und Portfoliostrukturierung, 9th edition. Stuttgart: Schäffer-Poeschel

Stern, W. C. and Deimler, M., S., 2006. The Boston Consulting Group: On Strategy. New Jersey: John Wiley & Sons

Stolzenberg, K. and Heberle, K., 2009. Change Management – Veränderungsprozesse erfolgreich mitgestalten. Heidelberg: Springer

Taleb, N. N., 2007. The Black Swan. London: Penguin Group

The Big Picture, 2008. Economist Debate on Regulation: Scholes vs. Stieglitz [online]. Thebigpicture.com. Available from: http://bigpicture.typepad.com/comments/2008/10/economist-debat.html [Accessed 4 February 2010]

The Economist (a), 2009. Efficiency and Beyond. The Economist, 18 July, 71 – 72. London: The Economist Group

The Economist (b), 2009. A special report on the carbon economy – Getting warmer. The Economist. 5 December 2009, 3 – 26. London: The Economist Group

The Economist (c), 2009. Briefing Fertility and living standards. The Economist, 29 – 32. London: The Economist Group

The Economist (e), 2009. An astonishing rebound. The Economist, 14 – 25. London: The Economist Group

The Economist (f), 2009. The world in 2010: Meek Oil. The Economist. 13 November 2009, 33 – 35. London: The Economist Group

The Economist (g), 2009. How to feed the world. The Economist. 21 November 2009, 13. London: The Economist Group

The Economist (j), 2009. The world in 2010: Reshaping the post-crisis world. The Economist. 13 November 2009, 20 – 32. London: The Economist Group

The Economist, 2009 (d). Better than nothing [online]. Economist.com. Available from: http://www.economist.com/world/international/PrinterFriendly.cfm?story_id=15124 802 [Accessed 24 December 2009]

The Economist, 2009 (h). Diversification [online]. Economist.com. Available from: http://www.economist.com/businessfinance/management/PrinterFriendly.cfm?stor y_id=14298922 [Accessed 5 February 2010]

The Economist, 2009 (i). Seking Compromise [online]. Economist.com. Available from: http://www.economist.com/sciencetechnology/PrinterFriendly.cfm?story_id=15106 331 [Accessed 6 February 2010]

The Free Dictionary, 2010. Definition of paradigm [online]. Thefreedictionary.com.
Available from: http://www.thefreedictionary.com/paradigm
[Accessed 4 February 2010]

Thompson, A., Strickland, A. J. and Gamble, E., 2008. Crafting and Executing
Strategy: The quest for competitive advantage, 16th edition. New York: McGraw
Hill

Turner, R. and Rauwald, C., 2008. Credit crunch threatens Europe's auto industry
[online]. DW-World.de. Available from: http://www.dw-
world.de/dw/article/0,,3753710,00.html [Accessed 5 February 2010]

United Nations (a), 2009. Climate Change Conference [online]. COP15.dk.
Available from: http://www.denmark.dk/en/menu/Climate-Energy/COP15-
Copenhagen-2009/cop15.htm [Accessed 18 November 2009]

United Nations (b), 2009. Statements by Supachai Panitchpakdi [online]. United
Nations Conference on Trade and Development. Available from:
http://www.unctad.org/TEMPLATES/Webflyer.asp?docID=11901&intItemID=3549
&lang=1 [Accessed 5 February 2010]

Van Horne, J. C. and Wachowicz, J. M., 2005. Fundamentals of Financial
Management, 12th edition. Essex: Prentice-Hall

Verweire, L. and van den Berghe, 2004. Integrated Performance Management,
London: Sage

von Düsterlho, J. E., 2003. Das Shareholder-Value Konzept. Wiesbaden: Gabler

Wagenhofer, A., 2006. Controlling und IFRS Rechnungslegung. Berlin: Erich
Schmidt Verlag

Wall, S. and Rees, B., 2004. International Business, 2nd edition. London: Pearson

Welfens, P. J. J., 1999. Globalization, Economic Growth and Innovation
Dynamics. Heidelberg: Springer

Wellner, K. and Pelzl, W., 2003. Entwicklung eines Immobilien Portfolio Systems,
Norderstedt: Books on Demand

Whittington, R., 2001. What is strategy - And does it matter?, 2nd edition. London:
Cengage

Wiehle, U., 2007. 100 IFRS Kennzahlen, 3rd edition. Wiesbaden: Cometis